The material in this book was originally devised and co-written by John Charter. Since its inception in the mid-1990s it has been run numerous venues by John Hardwick. John works under the banner of *Counties* and to present the Christian message in an exciting way, which will appeal to children of all ages. Equally well received in schools and churches, John's musical skills (both as a composer and performer) and his skills in storytelling, sometimes accomplished through juggling and unicycling, are a proven success. He is based in Cambridgeshire, but travels widely, leading praise parties, training sessions on creative communication and all-age worship. He is an all-age worship leader at Spring Harvest and Easter People.

John is a key member of the *Barnabas* freelance team and author of the popular holiday club resources *We're going on a Jungle Jamboree!*, *Champions!* and *Junior Heroes!*, all published by BRF.   -

Text copyright © John Hardwick 2008
Illustrations copyright © Simon Smith 2008
The author asserts the moral right
to be identified as the author of this work

Published by
Barnabas, an imprint of The Bible Reading Fellowship
15 The Chambers, Vineyard
Abingdon OX14 3FE
United Kingdom
Websites: www.brf.org.uk; www.barnabasinchurches.org.uk

ISBN 978 1 84101 545 3
First published 2008
10 9 8 7 6 5 4 3 2 1 0
All rights reserved

Acknowledgments
Unless otherwise stated, scripture quotations are taken from the Contemporary English Version of the Bible published by
HarperCollins Publishers, copyright © 1991, 1992, 1995 American Bible Society.

Scripture quotations taken from the Holy Bible, New International Version, copyright © 1973, 1978, 1984 by International
Bible Society, are used by permission of Hodder & Stoughton Publishers, a division of Hodder Headline Ltd. All rights reserved.
'NIV' is a registered trademark of International Bible Society. UK trademark number 1448790.

Scriptures quoted from the Good News Bible published by The Bible Societies/HarperCollins Publishers Ltd, UK © American
Bible Society 1966, 1971, 1976, 1992, used with permission.

Performance and copyright

The right to perform *The Starship Discovery Holiday Club* drama material is included in the purchase price, so long as the
performance is in an amateur context, for instance in church services, schools or holiday club venues. Where any charge is
made to audiences, written permission must be obtained from the author, who can be contacted through the publishers. A fee
or royalties may be payable for the right to perform the script in that context.

A catalogue record for this book is available from the British Library

Printed in Singapore by Craft Print International Ltd

The Starship Discovery Holiday Club!

A five-day holiday club plan, complete and ready-to-run

John Hardwick

This book is dedicated to my mate, Alan Charter, with whom I co-wrote the original version of Starship Discovery. *Alan uses his tremendous sense of humour when reaching children with the gospel, training children's workers and encouraging church leaders that children really do matter! I worked with him in the Saltmine children's team on the road for two years. It was great being able to serve the Lord together and have a laugh all at the same time. Alan has gone on to become the Head of Evangelism for Scripture Union and director of the web initiative,* Children Matter! *(www.childrenmatter.net). Alan wanted to write the Foreword to this book: he is delighted that I've had the opportunity to develop the theme further and that* Starship Discovery *will help to reach a new generation with God's love.*

Acknowledgments

With thanks to the following people for their help and inspiration:
My wife, Rachel, and children, Chloe and Ben.
Alan Charter, who co-wrote the original theme.
Paul Willmott, Ruth Wills and Phil Brown, who wrote the theme song.
Sue Doggett, my diligent editor.
Simon Smith, for his fantastic artwork.
David Wilkinson, for the sheet music.
Thanks also to St John's Woodbridge, Histon Holiday Club, St Neots Evangelical Church,
St Michaels Chelmsford and Godmanchester Holiday Club for allowing me
to try out my new themes on them and for helping with ideas.

Contents

Foreword

Having known John for more years than I care to mention, I am delighted to put fingers to keyboard to commend *The Starship Discovery Holiday Club!* to you. I would love to tell you how I had taught John everything he knows… but that would not be the case. What is the case is that I have learned a great deal from him over the years and have been encouraged by his passionate commitment to making the gospel of Jesus accessible to children.

The Starship Discovery Holiday Club! is a great tool to help you take children on that voyage of discovery for themselves. Journeying through the experience of Peter brings an unparalleled close encounter with the Master himself. The combination of a child's fascination for the wonder of space and the timeless truths of one man's life-transforming relationship with the creator of time and space itself gives you a wealth of creative possibilities. I hope that you will have as much fun preparing and running this programme as John and I did a few years back when we first worked on it.

Allow your imagination to run riot as you embark on this adventure together. The impression made on the life of a child can truly last for eternity. You will not always see all the fruit from the investment made by you, your church or a group of churches in your community, but be assured—there will be fruit. Never underestimate the impact upon the life of a child by those who combine a love for Jesus and a love for children. When Jesus states, 'When you welcome even a child because of me, you welcome me' (Mark 9:37), we are reminded that there is an unfathomable 'kingdom thing' going on when we go the extra mile to welcome children. It really is worth all the effort.

One more thing… to make this a true voyage of discovery, make sure you have put some thought into your next steps. There is a tremendous investment needed to pull off a week like this, so make sure you steward that commitment wisely. Look beyond the holiday club to the continuing ways you can make disciples of the children and their families. It is a high calling to work with children, as the impact of our ministry with them in these formational years is potentially lifelong.

Pray hard, give it your all and push on to that final frontier!

Alan Charter
Head of Evangelism, Scripture Union
www.scriptureunion.org.uk
Director, Children Matter!
www.childrenmatter.net

Introduction

The shepherd boy, David, looked up at the stars in the sky and was awestruck by what he saw. The night sky was the inspiration behind much of his worship, giving rise to words of praise such as 'I often think of the heavens your hands have made, and of the moon and stars you put in place' (Psalm 8:3), 'You spread out the sky like a tent…' (Psalm 104:2b) and 'Sun and moon, and all you bright stars, come and offer praise' (Psalm 148:3). Right from the beginning, after God had created the sun and the moon and flung stars into space, we humans have been fascinated by the vastness of God's creation. As our awareness has grown, we have marvelled at the incredible beauty of the stars and planets that make up not just our own solar system, but also the galaxies beyond our own—far beyond the extremities of our knowledge and understanding. In the last hundred years, people have reached out into space in new ways: people have walked on the moon and probes have explored distant planets.

Movie makers have produced many great films reflecting our love of space, such as *Flash Gordon*, *Star Wars*, *Star Trek*, *Lost in Space* and many more. At the time of writing, the latest favourite children's TV programme to hit the small screen is *Lunar Jim*. Jim follows in the footsteps of the classically popular series, *The Clangers*, and surely won't be the last to enthral the younger generation. With all this in mind, *The Starship Discovery Holiday Club!* is bang up to date and continues to be a perennially popular theme with children of all ages.

trip, the willingness to be *transformed* by Jesus and, finally, the willingness to *train* in our Christian faith, so that we are prepared for the journey ahead.

Using a mix of songs, warm-up activities, drama, crafts, games, puppet sketches, Bible narrations, quizzes and funsheets, the material offers five off-the-peg sessions, designed as a five-day holiday programme but equally suitable for midweek clubs and all-age worship. In addition, in Appendix One, you will find extra material that could be used for a special holiday club evening or a special all-age service as a conclusion to the holiday club itself.

Day 1: We first meet Peter when *he* first meets Jesus and chooses to give up everything to follow him. Choosing to follow Jesus is a big decision; it's not a short-term choice, but one that affects the rest of our lives.

Day 2: We next encounter Peter when he learns an important lesson about trust. Peter's trust took a big step when he tried to reach Jesus by walking on the water. When we keep our eyes on Jesus, he will hold us fast.

Day 3: Peter thought he would never let Jesus down, but circumstances proved differently. Peter shows us that we all make mistakes and, through him, we learn how Jesus dealt with the things Peter did (and we do) wrong.

Day 4: When Peter and the other disciples received the gift of God's Holy Spirit, they were transformed by the power that changed their lives.

Day 5: Finally, we see how God prepared Peter to be strong in times of trouble and how the power of prayer released him from prison. Despite being in prison, Peter's training stood him in good stead and he was prepared for the journey ahead.

Overview

The Starship Discovery Holiday Club! takes the ever-popular space theme to explore five characteristics of one of Jesus' closest friends—Peter, a fisherman and disciple. The framework for the material is five common spaceship images: 'Blast off!', 'Beam me up!', 'Black hole!', 'Breakthrough!' and 'Battle Stations!' At a second level, the material introduces five qualities common not just to Peter but also to Christians today. These five qualities are the willingness to *turn* towards Jesus, the willingness to *trust* Jesus, the humility to ask for forgiveness when we

Setting up

To create an outer space atmosphere, set the scene by having pictures and backdrops of stars and planets around the room. For reference, look for images on the Internet by typing "space and planets" into the search engine. You should instantly have hundreds of images that you can download and display around the room, build into PowerPoint slideshows, use to make a space quiz, or use as inspiration for your own ideas.

Choose space names for the children's teams, such as Stars, Milky Way, Moon, Mars, Jupiter, Saturn, Neptune, Pluto, Earth, Sun and so on, and arrange appropriate dress for your leaders and assistants. You'll need additional leaders to oversee the crafts and games, and a team leader to supervise the sessions.

Decorate your venue in keeping with the theme. The stage area could be made to look like a control desk in a spaceship. This is easily achieved by spraying a variety of household junk with silver spray paint and sticking it on to your backdrop. The rest of the holiday club area can be transformed with aluminium baking foil, as many flashing lights as you can find and pictures of stars, planets and galaxies.

Roles and responsibilities

Good teamwork is essential for good children's work. As well as an overall holiday club coordinator, you'll need people to fill all the following roles.

Registration officer

This role would suit a well-organized person. If the children are registered before the start date of the holiday club, you will save time on the first day of the club. If you choose to register the children on the first day, you will need a good team of helpers to cope with the workload.

You need to register the following details for each child. (See page 67 for a photocopiable registration form.)

- Name and address
- Date of birth
- Contact phone number
- Medical details (such as asthma or allergies)
- Parent's or guardian's permission for child to attend the club

You will need to split children into groups according to their age bands, and possibly sub-section them into teams. It's advisable to issue each child with a colour-coded sticker or badge to identify him or her and the team to which they belong. Have a 'welcome' team available 15 minutes before the start to make the children feel at home when they arrive.

Team leaders

Team leaders need to be able to deal with a high level of responsibility. Each team leader will be allocated to a particular group of children or age band. They will stay with the children the whole time, sitting with them and leading them through various activities. They will befriend, enthuse and maintain a level of control. It's important that team leaders join in the songs, as children will look to their leaders as role models.

Team helpers

These are people who can help the team leader. They need to be free to fetch things, accompany children to the toilet and so on. **NB:** Male leaders should not accompany female children to the toilet.

Games leader

This needs to be someone with experience of sorting children quickly, and accustomed to organizing games. A powerful voice would be an asset. Keep the games in one location and bring the children to that area when it is their turn to play.

Craft leader

This needs to be someone able to organize a simple craft activity. The craft leader will need to start collecting materials well in advance. Try to make the crafts theme-related. Once again, have a fixed location for crafts and bring the children to that area when it is their turn.

Time keeper

This person watches the time and gives a five-minute warning to activity leaders that the session is about to end. He or she then rings a bell when it's time for the teams to move on to the next activity.

Snack team

One person or team is needed to prepare drinks and biscuits for the children. Not all the children will need their drinks at the same time, as teams will take turns to have their refreshments. Please ensure that all the leaders, including the games leader and craft leader, also receive drinks.

First aider

It is essential to have someone available who is a trained first aider, and to have a well-stocked first aid box. St John Ambulance may be able to offer advice if you are unsure about how to provide this facility.

Discipler

Children may have questions about the Christian faith. Disciplers need to be able to talk in simple language and be good listeners. They should know what they believe and how to put it across without manipulation or forcing the children into making statements or promises that they cannot understand or keep.

You will need to think about how to follow up children who are seeking to know more about the Christian faith.

Publicity officer

This person is needed to design and organize posters, leaflets and school visits, and to contact the local press.

Floaters

Floaters are helpers who cannot commit themselves to attend the whole week's programme but are able to come for a day or two. They can help wherever there is a need.

Stage team or presenter

Either one person or a team is needed to lead the up-front programme, leading the songs, theme illustration, quiz, Bible story and teaching, and introducing the drama and puppet sketches. You may wish to fill this role from your own team, or you may decide to give your regular children's leaders a rest and bring in someone from outside.

Dos and don'ts

It's worth repeating that good children's work relies on good teamwork!

- Do sit with the children during upfront time.
- Do be prepared to join in the songs and interactive parts of the programme. Don't forget that children will

look to the team leaders as their role models.
- Do encourage, befriend and control your team of children.
- Do use your common sense.
- Do encourage children to go to the toilet during the activity times rather than the up-front/teaching times. Remember that children follow each other's lead: if you're not careful, all the young ones will decide at once that they need an outing to the toilet.
- Do expect to have fun yourself and be open to learn. The teaching aspect of the programme is not just for the kids—God may choose to speak to you, too.
- Don't loiter on the edge, chatting or distracting the children or presenter, as the programme is taking place.

Safety first

Agreed guidelines should be observed by everyone involved, in order to maintain the safety of the children and members of the team. Any questions relating to safety should be raised with the organizers before problems arise.

- No team member should be alone with a child where their activity cannot be seen by others.
- Always treat the children with respect and dignity.
- Never use physical punishment.
- Ensure that more than one person is present if a child needs to be washed or helped in the toilet.
- Don't become overfriendly, with children sitting on your lap, hugging, or rough-and-tumbling.
- Don't play-fight with children or join in games where you could fall on a child.
- Don't run around with children on your shoulders.

- Do not go into a room alone with a child, arrange to meet a child alone or invite a child to your home alone.
- Avoid any inappropriate touching or any excessively rough or physical games.
- Do not engage in any scapegoating, ridicule or rejection of a child.
- Avoid giving lifts to children. If a car journey is necessary, the child should sit on a rear seat, using an appropriate seat belt, and a second adult leader should be present.
- If you need to contact a child at home during or after the holiday club, ensure that you identify yourself as a member of the holiday club team.
- If abuse is suspected, do not encourage the child to talk further. Report suspicions immediately to the holiday club co-ordinator and make written notes of anything you and the child said to each other. **NB**: See websites listed below for further information.

Fire safety

- Do not use candles, matches or lighters on the premises.
- Familiarize yourself with the fire exits.
- Observe fire drills: they are for everybody's safety.

Stay legal

- If your holiday club lasts for more than two hours and runs for six days or more in a year, you need to register with Social Services. If you are planning follow-up events, this rule might affect you.
- If under-8s are involved, write to inform Social Services of your plans.
- Have someone on security to stop strangers from wandering in or children from wandering out.

For further information about legal requirements for child protection, contact your local council, your diocese or church office, or:

The Criminal Records Bureau
CRB Customer Services
PO Box 110, Liverpool L69 3EF
Tel: 0870 9090811
Website: www.crb.gov.uk

The Churches Child Protection Advisory Service
Disclosure Service
PO Box 133, Swanley, Kent BR8 7UQ
Telephone: 0845 120 4549
Fax: 0845 120 4552
E-mail:disclosure@ccpas.co.uk
Website: www.ccpas.co.uk

Incentives

Throughout our lives, we have incentives to help us achieve, or to keep up our enthusiasm and excitement for the job in hand. In schools, children have stars or house points and receive qualifications. In the workplace, there are company perks, plus the chance of promotion or a pay rise. Incentives can help with the boredom of routine. There is always a new target to reach.

At weekly children's clubs, incentives or a little competition can help to create and maintain enthusiasm, and there are many ways you can add them to the weekly programme. For example, with a personal achievement chart and/or team achievement score board, children can earn points that are visible on a card, scoring chart or token. They might earn points for:

- Attendance
- Answering a question in the quiz
- Being the coolest-behaved girl or boy
- Being outstanding at joining in activities
- Bringing along a friend

For your *Starship Discovery!* holiday club, the scoring chart could be based around the theme. For example:

- **Rocket launch**: Each child has their own rocket-shaped token, which they decorate and name. Create a 'launchpad' marked into divisions, like the rungs of a ladder. Each time a child wins a point, their rocket climbs up the launchpad ladder one rung at a time. (Stick the rockets to the chart with sticky tack.)
- **Shooting stars**: When a child wins a point, hand out a shooting star on which to write their name. (You can buy packs of card stars in fluorescent colours in stationery supply stores.) Using sticky tack, stick the named stars on a large backdrop. When a child reaches five stars, he or she receives a small prize—for example, a sweet. When a child reaches ten stars, he or she is given a bigger prize—for example, an item such as a pencil, yo-yo or badge.

You could continue the incentive by having a big prizegiving at the end of the holiday club and inviting parents along to it.

Equally, you could have a different chart or card for each day, or use tokens instead. If tokens are used, a child receives a token for the same reasons as before, which can be exchanged at the end of the day for a prize.

Try to avoid the 'tuck shop' idea where children can exchange their own money for sweets. Some children have plenty of money, while others have very little. It's far better to have a prize system where they all have an equal opportunity to earn a prize.

Daily programmes

Day 1: Blast off!

The theme for today is 'Turning'. Peter was just going about his daily life when he first met Jesus. In fact, in those days, his name wasn't even Peter—it was Simon. Jesus turned Simon Peter's life on its head and things were never the same again.

Bible story: Matthew 4:18–22; Mark 1:16–20 and Luke 5:1–11.
Memory verse: Choose yourself today whom you will serve; as for me, I will serve the Lord (based on Joshua 24:15, NIV).

Day 2: Beam me up!

The theme for today is 'Trusting'. When we follow Jesus, we have to learn to trust him, even when we do not know or understand what will happen. When Peter stepped out of the boat, above all he was taking a step of faith in which he needed to trust Jesus above everything else.

Bible story: Matthew 14:22–32; Mark 6:45–52 and John 6:15–21.
Memory verse: Trust in the Lord with all your heart and lean not on your own understanding (Proverbs 3:5, NIV).

Day 3: Black hole!

The theme for today is 'Tripping'. No matter how hard we try, none of us is perfect: we all make mistakes and do wrong things. Peter let Jesus down very badly, but his story helps us to understand how Jesus deals with the things we do to hurt him, others and ourselves.

Bible story: Matthew 26:69–75; Mark 14:66–72; Luke 22:56–62 and John 18:15–18, 25–27.
Memory verse: Christ Jesus came into the world to save sinners (1 Timothy 1:15).

Day 4: Breakthrough!

God has the power to transform our lives. Sometimes this happens gradually and sometimes it happens all at once, but, however the transformation takes place, Jesus promised that his Holy Spirit would be with us to strengthen and encourage us.

Bible story: Acts 2:1–47.
Memory verse: I will always be with you; I will never abandon you (Joshua 1:5b, GNB).

Day 5: Battle stations!

Whatever we do in life, we need to get into training if we want to do something well. We don't need to train to become Christians, but if we are serious about wanting to follow Jesus, we need to train to be prepared for the journey ahead. Prayer is our training ground and the means by which we can win battles for God.

Bible story: Acts 12:6–19.
Memory verse: We often suffer, but we are never crushed. Even when we don't know what to do, we never give up. In times of trouble, God is with us, and when we are knocked down, we get up again (2 Corinthians 4:8–9).

Starship Discovery! timetable

A two-and-a-half-hour programme (adaptable to suit your situation)

9.15am   Team meet together to pray.

9.35am   Last-minute preparation.

9.45am   Doors open for registration. Split the children into three teams according to their ages. Children go to team leaders/areas.

10.00am: Stage-based presentation/up-front time 1 (30 minutes):
- Introduction and welcome
- Opening talk to introduce the theme for the day
- Theme song (see page 13 for details)
- Action song
- Theme illustration or theme team challenge
- Memory verse song
- Watt family daily drama
- Song or Bible memory verse recap

10.30am: Activity time: three activities, each lasting for 25 minutes. In their teams, the children rotate round the different activities so that all the children do each activity:
- Game
- Craft
- Snack, chat and funsheet

12.00pm: Stage-based presentation/up-front time 2 (30 minutes):
- Songs
- Puppet sketch
- Bible memory verse recap
- Quick quiz
- Bible story
- Round-up/prayer
- Theme song

12.30pm: Children go back to small groups and wait to be collected.

Starship Discovery! theme song

Up there, out of this world, / rockets flying high / Up there, out of this world, / stars go shooting by / Up there, out of this world, / gazing up above / Up there, out of this world, God made it out of love. V.1 See moon and stars and a big black hole, but do you know who's in control? God, he made them one by one, 'cos his love and his power they go on and on and on and

Up there, out of this world,
Rockets flying high!
Up there, out of this world,
Stars go shooting by.
Up there, out of this world,
Gazing up above.
Up there, out of this world,
God made it out of love.

See moon and stars and a big black hole,
But do you know who's in control?
God, he made them one by one,
'Cos his love and his power,
They go on and on and on and…

Up there, out of this world…

See galaxies and nebulae,
Ever stopped to wonder why?
God loves us, loves everyone,
'Cos his love and his power,
They go on and on and on and…

Up there, out of this world…

The Watt Family theme song

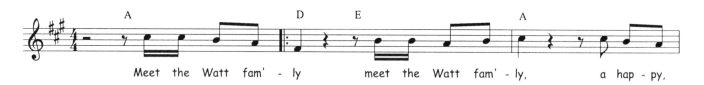

Meet the Watt fam' - ly   meet the Watt fam' - ly,   a hap - py,

wack - y, cra - zy, ord - in - ar - y fam - i - ly.   Meet the Watt fam' - ly,   meet the Watt fam' -

ly,   a lov - ing, car - ing, shar - ing, ord - in - ar - y fam - i - ly.   Meet the Watt fam' - ly.

Starship Discovery! Bible memory verse songs

Although the following verses are based on actual Bible texts, they do not necessarily include the whole verse, and wording may vary slightly to fit the melody.

―――――――――――― **Day One: Blast off!** ――――――――――――

Choose yourself

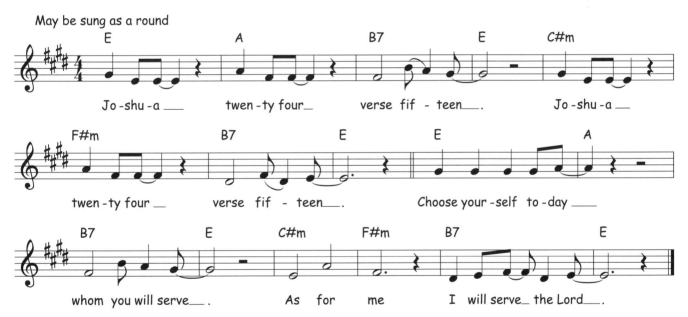

May be sung as a round

Jo-shu-a ___ twen-ty four ___ verse fif-teen ___. Jo-shu-a ___ twen-ty four ___ verse fif-teen ___. Choose your-self to-day ___ whom you will serve ___. As for me I will serve ___ the Lord ___.

Trust in the Lord

Christ Jesus came

First Ti -mo - thy (echo) chap -ter one (echo) verse fif - teen__. First Ti -mo -

thy (echo) chap -ter one (echo) verse fif - teen__. Christ Je -sus__came

in -to the world to save sin -ners__. Christ Je -sus__came in -to the world

to save__ sin -ners__. That means you, that means me.

None of us are per -fect you've got to a -gree__, that means you, that means

me. Je - sus who is per -fect died____ for you and me!

I will always be with you

Jo-shu-a___ chap-ter one___ verse___ five___. I will al-ways

be with_ you___. I will al-ways be with_ you___. I will ne-ver, ne-

- ver a-ban-don_ you___, I will ne-ver, ne - ver a-ban-don_ you___.

We are on the victory side

Opening talks

Start each day of your holiday club with a short talk to help set the scene and introduce the theme. Use the Internet to find images to illustrate your talk: there are lots to choose from, including pictures of planets, rockets, space shuttles, aeroplanes, images of the world taken from space, and so on. You could build the images into a PowerPoint slideshow as a background to your talk, but do keep everything short—five minutes maximum.

Day One: Blast off!

Turning

Welcome to Starship Discovery! I wonder if you have ever been outside on a clear night and looked up at the night sky. On a clear night you can see the moon, thousands of stars and the vastness of space. There have been lots of films and TV programmes about space. *(Ask the children which ones they know about or have seen.)* Yes, *Lost in Space* and *The Clangers* were on TV when I was a kid, and so were *Star Trek* and *Dr Who*. There were also big films such as *Star Wars* and *ET*. Nowadays, characters such as *Lunar Jim* are very popular, and I'm sure you can think of loads more. All these are, of course, only made-up stories, and the spaceships are just models. But in our time we have real rockets and satellites, too—and even the space shuttle, a spacecraft that goes into space and back again.

I wonder if you have ever wished that you could travel into space. Once upon a time, space travel would have been just that—wishful thinking. But in 1969 the rocket spacecraft Apollo 11 took three astronauts to the moon, and Neil Armstrong and Edwin 'Buzz' Aldrin became the first people ever to walk on its surface. These guys actually *chose* to become astronauts and go to the moon, even though they didn't know what would happen there or even if they would make it back home. But, wow, what an adventure it turned out to be when they decided to turn themselves towards the possibility of going to the moon! Life would never be the same again. Can you imagine how fantastic it would have been to walk on the moon and see the earth from outer space? But, even though it was the most exciting thing they would ever do, Buzz Aldrin was a Christian and he said that people walking on the moon was nowhere near as important as when God walked on the earth.

This week we're going to have our own outer space adventure. There's lots of fun on our journey ahead, with games, songs, crafts and puppets. We'll be meeting the Watt family and joining in their adventure in space, but, most of all, we'll be finding out why God walking on the earth is the most important event ever to happen in the history of the world. So let's start our journey of discovery! *(Follow the talk with the Starship Discovery! theme song.)*

Day Two: Beam me up!

Trusting

Put your hand up if you have ever been on an aeroplane. I can remember the first time I flew in an aeroplane. I remember sitting down and putting on my seat belt and listening to the safety instructions. I remember thinking, 'Can this huge chunk of metal really get into the air and stay there? Is it really possible?' Then the engines started roaring and the aeroplane was shaking and suddenly it sped off down the runway and somehow lifted up into the sky. I was flying!

In order to fly in an aeroplane, I have to trust a lot of people. I have to trust the person who invented the aeroplane, the engineers who designed it and the pilot at the controls. I have to trust that they know how an aeroplane takes off, flies and lands safely. I don't really know about or understand any of these things—I just know that it works and that, apparently, flying is the safest way to travel.

In the same way, we may not understand everything about God. We may not understand how he created the world or designed us—but God wants us to trust him to be at the controls of our lives. All we need to know is that he is kind and loves us very much.

So let's start on a journey of trust today as we hear about how Simon Peter trusted Jesus in a very special way! *(Follow the talk with the Starship Discovery! theme song.)*

Day Three: Black hole!

Tripping

Did you know that planet earth (that's our planet) is exactly the right distance from the sun for life to exist? Mercury and Venus are just too hot, whereas Uranus and the dwarf planet, Pluto, are just too cold. But planet earth is just right for life. Our world is beautiful, full of life and energy.

It says in the Bible that God wants us to take care of planet earth—the world he has given us to live in. But we haven't done a very good job of looking after God's fantastic world. Sometimes people hunt animals just for fun, every day we destroy more and more of the rainforests, which are so important to the life and health of our world, and sometimes we hurt each other. Each one of us lets God down in the way we think and behave, but God knows when we trip up and he wants to put it right. Today, we're going to hear a story about how Simon Peter let Jesus down big time, and see what Jesus did about that. So let's get started on our journey of discovery and find out how Jesus forgives us and loves us—even when we trip up! *(Follow the talk with the Starship Discovery! theme song.)*

Day Four: Breakthrough!

Transforming

Did you know that your great-great-great-grandparents couldn't just drive to the airport, jump on an aeroplane and fly off to another country like many of us can today? Why not? Well, cars hadn't been invented, nor had aeroplanes, so there were no such things as airports!

People had been trying to fly for years. First of all, they built huge wings and strapped them to their bodies like the wings of a bird. Then they tried to fly by flapping their wings—but people aren't strong enough to lift their body weight off the ground in the way that birds can. Many people were killed trying to fly like that.

Then, on 17 December 1903, there was a breakthrough. The Wright brothers had been trying to build a flying machine for years and years, and then, finally, they built a plane that stayed in the sky for 12 seconds and flew 36 metres! That may not seem very long, but they had done it—they had built the first flying machine. The world was transformed, and it has never been the same since.

Today's Bible story is the most exciting story ever in the history of the world. It's about how God can transform our lives with the gift of his Holy Spirit. It's a real breakthrough, and people's lives are still being transformed even today.

So let's get started on our journey of discovery and find out more about the amazing gift that God gives to everyone who wants to follow Jesus! *(Follow the talk with the Starship Discovery! theme song.)*

Day Five: Battle stations!

Training

If you want to fly an aeroplane or a spaceship into outer space, you need to have training. Even if you think you'd be good at it, you still won't be able to do it if you don't train. Training prepares us for the journey ahead.

Lots of films about space adventures include battles in which people fight against alien forces. These are just made-up stories, but they remind us that there are forces in real life that stop us being the people God wants us to be. We need to prepare our battle stations and get into training so that we can fight for what is right when bad things come along.

In today's Bible story, we're going to hear how Peter and his friends kept going when things went very wrong. Peter and his friends had trained for the day when they would have to fight against enemy forces and we'll see from the story that when we are on God's side, we are on the victory side.

So let's get started on today's journey of discovery and find out how we can get into training for God! *(Follow the talk with the Starship Discovery! theme song.)*

Theme illustrations and challenges

Children love being volunteers, so here is an opportunity for them to be involved, have fun and learn something all at the same time. For each day, you have the choice of either a team challenge or a theme illustration: choose the one to suit your club. These activities work better if the volunteers are older children.

If you choose to have a team challenge, be aware that they can absorb a lot of your upfront time, so keep them tightly controlled. You may wish to prime volunteers beforehand by having a challenge box. The children who want to be involved in a challenge put their name and team in the box; you choose them before the day starts and call out their names at the appropriate moment. This can save valuable time. Do warn your volunteers that they may get a little wet! If you need team leaders to act as volunteers, choose these people beforehand, too.

away from other decisions we could have made instead. Even when we decide to turn towards a certain course of action, things don't always turn out how we expect.

Ask the volunteers, one at a time, to pick up and open the packet they 'turned towards'. Get them to empty the contents into a glass bowl. As the children open the packets they have chosen, ask them if they were surprised to find out what was inside. Was it what they were expecting? Produce the unopened packet. What do the children think is inside it?

Today we are looking at the theme of what it means to turn towards something, and later in the story we will meet someone who turned and made a choice that turned out to be more amazing than they ever expected. When we turn towards Jesus and make the decision to follow him, things may not turn out quite as we expected, but we will face life's unexpected surprises together with him.

Day One: Blast off!

Turning: Theme illustration

Buy a variety pack of cereals. Beforehand, open the bottom of every packet except one and empty out the contents. Then refill the packets with different 'surprises', such as sweets, dried lentils, scraps of paper, a 10p coin or a balloon. Leave one packet empty.

Display the packets on a table (making sure you keep back the unopened packet) and ask for volunteers to come and point towards their favourite packet. Talk about the choices that we all have to make every day. Some are simple choices, but others are more difficult. When we make decisions, we need to turn towards that decision and turn

Turning: Team challenge

In preparation, set up a small obstacle course (round a chair, over a small table, under a sheet or net and so on). You will also need one blindfold for each team.

Take two volunteers from each team and blindfold one of each pair. The blindfolded volunteer should be set to face in the opposite direction to the obstacle course. The one who isn't blindfolded has to guide his or her partner down the course by calling directions, but, of course, the first job is to direct the partner to turn round. This is not as easy as it seems, because the person who is blindfolded doesn't even know where the course starts. This challenge works well as a race but, if you don't have the space, let each team take it in turns and record the time taken.

God wants to guide us in our lives, but first of all we must make the decision to turn towards him. To do this, we need to recognize that we get things wrong and say 'sorry' for the wrong things we do. We can then change the direction of our lives and follow God's directions rather than our own.

Day Two: Beam me up!

Trusting: Theme illustration

You need an older volunteer or a young leader and you need to be a strong catcher. Ask your volunteer if they trust you. If the answer is 'yes', ask them to stand up straight with their back to you, as you want them to fall back into your arms without bending their legs. Tell them that you will not let them down (so don't!).

When your volunteer has done it once, blindfold them (or you could use another volunteer if you wish) and ask them again to fall back into your arms. Then, without moving the blindfold, say that you want to do it a third time. As you are saying this, move in front of the volunteer so that they can hear that your voice is no longer behind them. Prime another strong leader to sneak quietly behind the volunteer and, with the leader in position, ask the volunteer to fall back once more. They will hesitate as they are now confused about who will catch them. Say again (while standing in front of them) that they can trust you: you won't let them fall.

It's easy to trust when we know what is going on, but when we don't know what the future holds, it can be very difficult. God wants us to trust him. He won't let us down.

Trusting: Team challenge

This challenge is called 'The flying saucer race'. In preparation, you need to buy some packets of flying saucer sweets (the sherbet-filled sugar-paper sweets that you can buy from most supermarkets or sweetshops). You also need a packet of straight drinking straws. Cut the straws in half so that each straw makes two short straws: each child will need one of these short straws. Place one small dish or bowl per team at one end of the playing area. Fill each bowl with flying saucer sweets. Place one chair per team at the opposite end of the playing area.

This is a relay race that requires each team to work together and trust each other. Each team stands in a line between the bowl and the chair. The last person in line sits on the chair facing their team and opens their mouth, waiting to receive the flying saucer sweet. When you say 'Go!' the person nearest the bowl picks up a flying saucer sweet from the bowl by sucking it on to the end of a straw. They then turn to the next person, who touches their

straw to the other side of the flying saucer sweet and secures it to the straw by sucking. (The first person needs to stops sucking at this point!) This continues down the line until the sweet reaches the last person in the line, who turns and pops the sweet into the mouth of the person sitting on the chair. That person then runs to the front of the line and the one now at the end of the line sits on the chair. The game continues until time is called.

The winning team is the team that ate the most flying saucers in the allocated time of, say, one and a half minutes. The challenge can be played with three children in each team, but more can join in if time allows.

After the challenge has been completed, explain that it's important to work together. There is nothing more important than to be able to trust those around you. God also wants you to trust him.

Day Three: Black hole!

Tripping: Theme illustration

The theme illustration today takes the form of a short sketch called 'The message of the cross'. For the sketch, you will need either some chalk and a small handheld blackboard on which to draw as the sketch is performed, or small laminated signs, which you have prepared beforehand. The sketch is performed by two leaders.

Leader 1: When I was a kid I used to think my teacher loved me!

Leader 2: Loved you?

Leader 1: Yeah, she used to put kisses all over my work. *(Draws or shows a big X)*

Leader 2: That's not a kiss. That means you got it w-r-o-n-g! The cross means you got it w-r-o-n-g!

Leader 1: Yes, I know that now—but it was very confusing at the time. Then, when I was a teenager, I had my first Valentine's card. It said, 'I think you are really cute!'

Leader 2: Oh, how sweet!

Leader 1: Not really, because it then had three Xs. So what it really said was, 'I think you are really cute! Wrong, wrong, wrong!'

Leader 2: No, that means your secret admirer loved you and wanted to give you a kiss.

Leader 1: Yuck! So what you're saying is that Xs mean w-r-o-n-g, but also mean l-o-v-e?

Leader 2: That's right!

Leader 1: Yes, but when I was 18 years old and allowed to vote, I went into the voting booth and I had to put an X next to the name of the person I wanted to vote for. I got really confused because I couldn't work out whether the X was to say that I thought they were wrong, or to say that I loved them. So I read the instructions again, and it said to put a cross next to the person you choose.

Leader 2: That's right! X also means something you choose! This little symbol, 'X', has several different meanings.

Leader 1: Yeah. It reminds me of Easter.

Leader 2: Easter?

Leader 1: Yeah, Christians believe Jesus died on the cross because of all the w-r-o-n-g things we have done! *(Shows or draws a cross)*

Leader 2: Oh yeah!

Leader 1: And he died on the cross because he l-o-v-e-s us! *(Shows or draws a second cross)*

Leader 2: Of course!

Leader 1: But he didn't have to die on the cross: he c-h-o-s-e to die that way because he loves us! *(Shows or draws a third cross)* Also, Christians believe that God wants us to c-h-o-o-s-e to follow him. So that little 'X' describes what a Christian is!

Leader 2: I see what you mean. A Christian is someone who knows that they have done w-r-o-n-g, but also knows that God l-o-v-e-s them and then c-h-o-o-s-e-s to follow Jesus. What a great symbol the X is!

Tripping: Team challenge

Beforehand, you need to prepare a black slime dip for each team, to represent a black hole. To make a black slime dip, fill a see-through container, such as a large sweet container or a small fish bowl, three-quarters full of water. Turn the water black with black food colouring or gravy browning. Add some ingredients such as flour, cornflour, baked beans, tinned fruit salad or porridge oats to give the dip a thick, slimy consistency. Stir three 'precious' items, such as chocolate coins wrapped in clingfilm, into each slime dip.

Ask each member of each team to plunge their hand into their team's slime dip for 30 seconds to find the precious items. The winner is the team that finds all their precious items first. Alternatively, you could have one slime dip and give volunteers 30 seconds each to see how many precious items they can find.

After the challenge has been completed, explain that today's theme is all about the times when we seem to go into black holes—times when we trip up and know that we have done something wrong. We are going to hear about how Peter tripped up just at the time when Jesus needed him most. Jesus went through a terrible black hole for us because each one of us is so precious to God—and he forgives each one of us when we get things wrong, just as he forgave Peter.

Day Four: Breakthrough!

Transforming: Theme illustration

Have ready the largest torch you can find. Proudly show the children your large and powerful torch. Say how wonderful it is in the dark. It has a powerful beam that shines right into the sky; it can shine on someone a long away off and brighten their path. Switch on the torch to show them how good it is—but it doesn't seem to work. My wonderful torch doesn't work! Have someone primed to come on stage with a gift for you. You excitedly open the gift, but you are a little disappointed to discover that it's just a battery. Someone suggests you put it in the torch—and suddenly the torch works perfectly.

A torch without a battery is still a torch, but the power—the energy—is missing, so it's not much good. In the same way that a torch needs a battery, we need God in our lives. He becomes part of our lives by giving us the gift of his Holy Spirit. All we need to do is to invite him in. He is like a light shining inside us. He comforts us when things go wrong and gives us courage to speak out for him and do what is right.

Transforming: Team challenge

Ask for two volunteers from each team. You want to see how creative they are and how good their team is at making the right choice. Give each team a large piece of paper. One volunteer will have to build a paper aeroplane and the other must throw it as far as they can. Their team has to choose who they think will make the best aeroplane (the designer) and who will be the best thrower (the pilot). Once the choice has been made for each team, the designer will have one minute to make an aeroplane. Then each team's pilot will take turns to throw their aeroplane. The one that gets the furthest is the winner.

After the challenge, point out that an ordinary plain piece of paper was transformed into something special just by folding it in a certain way. In the same way, God transforms us, even though we are just ordinary people. If we give him our lives, he starts to work on us, transforming us into the people he wants us to be.

Day Five: Battle stations!

Training: Theme illustration

Have ready some relighting candles. Light the candles in front of the children and explain how God brings light into our lives. Go on to say that there are many things, or even people, that will 'knock us back' in our lives, even when we journey with God. Invite someone to blow out the candles (if it's someone's birthday, you could choose that person). The candle should go out for a second but then burst back into life.

Explain that, despite the knockback, the light keeps returning and burning as brightly as ever. In our lives there will be many tough times and knockbacks, but God is always there and will help us to bounce back. His light will always continue to shine.

Training: Team challenge

Beforehand, prepare the challenge by rolling up lots and lots of pieces of paper to make paper balls (meteorites) and have ready some water pistols or bubble guns (space guns). Set up an obstacle course. You will also need an egg and spoon. Boil the egg in advance if you don't want to have to clear up the mess.

Take three volunteers from each team. One volunteer from each team will carry the precious cargo (the egg on the spoon) through the obstacle course, but the other volunteers will make it even more difficult for their opponents by throwing the meteorites and shooting the space guns at them. The winner is the one to makes it to the end of the course first without dropping the precious cargo. If they drop the cargo, they have to go back to the start.

Can the people carrying the precious cargo keep going with so much going on around them? How determined are they to be on the victory side? Life can be difficult when you are a Christian. Sometimes people make fun of you and even try to stop you from believing in God. How determined are you to be on God's victory side? He will be there to help you, so don't give up. Be a winner!

The Watt family daily dramas

This is a five-part contemporary story that picks up the space theme, revealing it in daily instalments. The story outline can be adapted to be performed as a drama or dramatic narration, or read as a story. Feel free to embellish and adapt the scripts to suit your own situation. Play the Watt family theme tune as the cast comes on stage and again at the end of the drama.

Drama tips

Many of the following tips can be useful for those telling the Bible narrations, too.

- Start practising a good month or two before the holiday club. I recommend a minimum of six one-hour practices. The first practice will involve choosing who will play which character and reading through the whole script to get into the storyline plot. You may choose to record this read-through and make copies for each member of the cast. This is a good technique for learning lines quickly.

- Project your voice: speak out loud and clear. Don't turn your back to the audience when speaking. It is better to face the audience and turn your head to the side when speaking to another character.

- A technician can be useful. Background music or sound effects can add to the atmosphere, but don't make them so loud that the actors can't be heard.

- If you are playing the part of a baddie, try to be a nice, cheeky baddie rather than a very loud, aggressive one. Little children scare easily.

- Don't rush lines. Often, jokes are lost because the delivery isn't clear. I've tried to keep the script short to make it easy to learn, but you need to make the Watt family come to life through plenty of movement. It is useful if someone with experience in drama can come to your rehearsals to watch and direct you in the delivery of lines and stage blocking. Constructive criticism can help to bring the drama to life.

- Think about movement, facial expression, entrances and exits. If there is a chase scene, work out a routine and decide whether you need to have some 'chase' music playing in the background. Often, children find this type of humour funnier than the actual lines.

- Think about your set and costumes. Don't leave costumes and props to the last minute. Don't forget your local toyshop, costume shop and charity shop in your search for the right costumes and props. The Internet is also a good place to look for specific items such as bubble guns, fancy dress and sound effects.

Overview

The Watt family drama is based on pantomime style. The storyline adheres lightly to the main daily themes, but the intention is not to draw too strong a parallel; just have fun and make sure your audience does, too.

The action takes place on board the *Starship Discovery*. The narrator plays the part of the onboard computer. You could have the person playing this part sitting behind a screen (made from cardboard) so that only their face is visible (in the style of the TV programme *Red Dwarf*). Equally, the computer could be just a voice offstage coming through the PA system. If you choose this route, it is helpful for the computer (narrator) to be able to see the action.

Staging

To set the stage for the drama, you need a space-style control panel. This could be made out of cardboard boxes, painted in metallic colours. It adds an exciting dimension if you can create your own teleport. To do this, you will need three sheets of transparent rigid plastic sheeting, each measuring 600mm x 2000mm, and four planed strips of 50mm x 50mm timber, each measuring 600mm. From the wood, form a 600mm square on the floor at the back of your set on which to build the teleport. Drill clearance holes in the plastic sheets and screw them to the wooden strips on the three outwardly visible sides. Tape the vertical edges of the plastic sheets together with gaffer tape. The rear, fourth side needs to back on to a black curtain, which will allow your actors to slip through unseen by the audience.

To make your characters appear or disappear, you will need to hire a smoke machine. (Ensure with your supplier that the smoke used is non-toxic.) Position the smoke machine out of sight at the base of the teleport. The machine will need its own operator, who can fill the teleport with smoke at the appropriate moment. For added effect, instal a flashing light and use a sound effects CD to provide the spaceship's engine noise, computer noises and general 'space' atmospheric sounds. Make sure that your sound effects are kept to a suitable level so that the actors can still be heard.

Cast
★ Computer (The narrator and mainframe support to the cast)
★ Rick Watt (An untidy, adventure-mad and headstrong young lad)
★ Wendy Watt (Rick's very talkative and slightly annoying sister)
★ Mummy Watt (Keeps everything, and everyone, shipshape and in order)
★ Grandma Watt (Agile, yet eccentric; amazingly scatty for someone so wise)
★ Herbert Tarragon (An alien from outer space)

Props
★ Mobile phone (for Wendy)
★ Computer joystick (for Rick)
★ Cleaning materials, such as spray polish and feather duster (for Mummy)
★ Knitting (for Grandma)
★ A mop dressed up to look like Grandma Watt (for Day 2)
★ Sound effect CD of engine noises (roaring and taking off)
★ Sound effect CD of computer noise and general outer space noises
★ 'Chase' music

Day One: Blast off!

Computer: Space… it's really big out there! This is the computer's log of *Starship Discovery*, star date *(today's date)*. Our mission—to explore the distant reaches of the universe and seek out new planets as yet undiscovered. The computers on board the ship have been scanning a planet known as Earth to find a crew suitable for such a mission. All the data received has been analysed and some suitable crew members were found—but unfortunately they were busy, so we got… the Watt family!

Chosen for this special mission, for his youthful energy, modern approach and his skill at telling awful jokes, is Rick Watt. As you can see, he's a Nintendo sort of chap—yes, we were looking for the ideal pilot, but Rick will have to do.

Rick: *(Comes on full of enthusiasm and curiosity)* Radical! Look at this! Wow! What does this do? Where's the start button?

Computer: Don't touch that! Leave it alone!

Rick: *(Spinning round)* Who said that? Wendy, is that you?

Computer: Chosen for her intelligence, her linguistic skills (that means she talks a lot) and her amazing insight, our communications officer… Wendy Watt.

Wendy: Oooooh, very nice!

Rick: Hey, Wendy, look at this!

Wendy: Don't touch any buttons, you might do something silly…

Computer: Chosen for her excellent skills in domestic engineering (that mean she's a good cook, a nifty cleaner and has the ability to keep things shipshape), as we say in computer terms, a DTP—a Drastically Tidy Person—Mummy Watt!

Mummy: Oh, Rick! I've found you at last. I've been looking for you everywhere. You haven't made your bed this morning and your bedroom's a tip. You've left washing powder all over the kitchen floor and orange peel on the table, and… *(She breaks off)* My goodness, what a mess this place is! I will have to clean it up. *(She starts dusting)*

Computer: Now, to cap it all, the brains behind the mission, bringing wisdom and experience to the crew, with a crystal-clear sense of direction and the ability to outknit any challenger… It's Grandma Watt!

Grandma: Has anybody seen my cup of tea?

Reproduced with permission from *The Starship Discovery Holiday Club!* published by BRF 2008 (978 1 84101 545 3)

Computer:	Assume positions ready for take-off. Ten… nine… eight… seven… six… five… four… three… two… one… blast off! *(Sound effects of the roar of engines, such as an aeroplane starting up its engine)*
	As the Starship Discovery takes off, the whole cast shakes, swaying from side to side together. Grandma is busy trying to knit while nattering to Rick, whose piloting technique bears a close resemblance to someone playing a computer game. Mummy is busy trying to clean and is humming to herself. Wendy is trying to talk on her mobile phone.
Rick:	Hey, everyone, we've made it! We're in outer space.
Grandma:	Cool! How exciting! Where did you say we were? Can you just drop me off at the supermarket? I need to get some eggs.
Rick:	We're in outer space, Grandma.
Grandma:	*(A little confused)* Where's that? I've lived round here for years, but I've never heard of that place.
Rick:	Up in the sky, with the stars.
Grandma:	Oh, how nice. Argh! I've just remembered—I'm scared of heights!
Wendy:	Slow down, Rick! Are you sure you're going the right way?
Mummy:	What a mess! *(She wanders over to the teleport and steps inside to clean it)*
Rick:	I know what I'm doing, Wendy. Stop interfering! Turn on the space TV, will you? I want to see when *(current TV programme)* is on.
Wendy:	That's all you ever think about!
	Wendy presses the teleport button, thinking it's the space TV. As she does this, there is a noise and the teleport fills with smoke. No one notices that Mummy has disappeared.
Rick:	Mummy! Mummy! What's for lunch?
Wendy:	Typical! You're already thinking of your stomach.
Grandma:	Yes, daughter dear, what is for lunch?
Wendy:	I must admit, I am hungry too. What is for lunch, Mummy?
Rick:	Ha! Now who is thinking of their stomach?
Wendy:	*(Calling)* Mummy?
Grandma:	*(Calling)* Daughter, dear?
Rick:	Mummy? Where are you? Are you playing hide and seek?
Grandma:	Stop messing around, dear! Come out,

	come out, wherever you are. We need our lunch!
Computer:	She has been transported to an alien ship.
Wendy:	How did she get there?
Computer:	You pressed the teleport button while she was cleaning it.
Wendy:	Oh no, I didn't!
Computer:	Oh yes, you did!
Wendy:	Oh no, I didn't. *(She begins to cry)*
Computer:	Oh yes, you did! When Rick asked you to switch on the TV, you pressed the teleport button by mistake, and now she's been transported to the alien ship, Tarragon!
Grandma:	Tarragon? Sounds like a herb to me!
Computer:	The Tarragons are a bunch of aliens we know very little about. For all we know, they may like nothing better than blasting people into outer space.
Grandma:	Don't panic! Don't panic! *(Everyone panics)* No, no! I said, 'Don't panic'! Relax! *(Everyone stops panicking immediately and relaxes)*
Rick:	*(He panics again)* Hang on! How can we save her?
Wendy:	*(She panics again)* Will we ever see her again?
Grandma:	*(Panics)* Who will keep Rick and Wendy out of trouble?
Rick/Wendy:	Who will keep Grandma under control?
Computer:	But, worst of all, who will cook the dinner? Find out in the next exciting episode of… the Watt family!
	Play the Watt family theme tune as actors exit.

Day Two: Beam me up!

Computer:	Space… it's really big out there! If you remember, in our last exciting episode Wendy Watt accidentally transported her Mummy to the alien Tarragon spaceship. Oh dear, oh dear, what are they going to do?
Grandma:	Oh dear, oh dear, what are we going to do?
Wendy:	Yes, oh dear, what are we going to do?
Rick:	I've got a great idea! We could play on the PlayStation all day.
Grandma:	That is a good idea.
Wendy:	Stop it, both of you. This isn't a joke. For all we know, these aliens may be man-eating monsters.
Grandma:	I once saw a man-eating chicken.

Rick:	*(To Grandma)* Scary!
Grandma:	Not really, dear, it was just your grandfather having his Sunday lunch. But Wendy's right—what we need is a rescue plan.

All look as though they are thinking. Suddenly Rick looks up with finger in air as though he has an idea; others look on, ready to listen. Then he frowns and shakes head: he hasn't got an idea after all. Then Grandma does the same, but she hasn't an idea either.

Rick:	*(Jumps up with great excitement)* I've got it! *(Others look on, anticipating a great plan)*
Wendy:	Well, what is it?
Rick:	*(Pause)* My chewing gum. I lost it yesterday, but now I've found it stuck to the bottom of my pocket. *(He mimes pulling it out and putting it in his mouth)*
Grandma:	Yuck! *(Crossly)* You big banana! We thought you'd come up with a rescue plan.
Wendy:	I have! Why didn't I think of it before? Let's phone up the Tarragons and ask them for our Mummy back.
Rick:	Don't be daft, Wendy! Your mobile phone won't work in outer space. It's only a cheap one.
Computer:	Ahem…
Wendy:	Do you think our computer could link up with theirs?
Rick:	Worth a try…

They all crowd around the computer and read the screen.

Grandma:	Use Google, dear, to find a list of Tarragons. Here we are…
Wendy:	Chicken Tarragon…
Rick:	Herbert Tarragon…
Grandma:	Tarragon sauce…
Wendy:	Tarragon soup…
Rick:	Alien space ship Tarragon *(Everyone misses it)*
Grandma:	Tarragon dumplings… *(Computer interrupts)*
Computer:	You've found it—that's the one!
Grandma:	What, Tarragon dumplings?
Computer:	No, no, no, the one before… Alien space ship Tarragon. I'll send a message… Gosh, that was quick! They must have a powerful broadband system. The answer is 'No! You can't have Mummy Watt back!' Apparently, their spaceship has never

	been so tidy and they love her shepherd's pie… just a bit concerned about the shepherd.
Grandma:	What are you going on about?
Rick:	Tell them we'll blast them out the sky if they don't… *(Computer interrupts again)*
Computer:	Not a good idea. They have more advanced weapons than ours.
Wendy:	Anyway, Mummy's on board!
Computer:	*(In an excited voice)* Ha, I've got it! I'll contact them again. *(Make computer noises)* I've done it; they've agreed. She's just collecting her things.
Grandma:	Wow! Computer, I'm impressed! What did you say to them?
Computer:	Nothing much, I just said we'll do them a swap for a more advanced model.
Grandma:	What a great idea. But I didn't know we had a more advanced model.
Computer:	Oh yes, we have! It's called the super Grandma Watt deluxe.
Grandma:	Same name as me!
Computer:	It *is* you!
Rick:	Great idea! You're planning to swap Grandma with Mummy.
Wendy:	Yes, Mummy's a much better cook.
Grandma:	*(Looking most upset)* Thanks a lot.
Computer:	No, you don't understand. Look in the teleport.

Wendy opens the door and finds a mop dressed to look like Grandma.

Wendy:	Grandma! It's an exact likeness.
Grandma:	I think it's time I had my hair done.
Computer:	Now put it back in the teleport and we'll swap it for Mummy Watt. Push the teleport button, Rick!

Smoke fills the teleport and Mummy Watt appears.

All:	It worked! Hooray!
Computer:	Oh dear, red alert, red alert! *(Klaxon sounds)* Red alert! Red alert! The Tarragons are not happy. They are charging their weapons. *(All actors freeze)*

   Is there any way out? Will the Tarragons blast the Watt family to smithereens? Find out in the next exciting episode of… the Watt family!

Play the Watt family theme tune as actors exit.

Reproduced with permission from *The Starship Discovery Holiday Club!* published by BRF 2008 (978 1 84101 545 3)

Day Three: Black hole!

Computer: Space… it's really big out there! But not big enough, I'm afraid. I have upset the Tarragons by trying to fob them off with a mop, hoping they would think it was Grandma Watt. But they weren't taken in by my dastardly plan and now they are trying to blast us out of space. No time to talk to you. Quick, Rick, you need to be slick, Rick, if we are to escape. You need to pilot this ship like Luke Skywalker!

Rick: Who?

Rick, who is sitting down with the joystick controller, steers frantically, making revving engine noises. The others are standing up and overbalance as the space ship accelerates.

Computer: Follow my instructions, Rick. It's going to take some ducking and diving. Ready? To the left… *(All the cast lean and stumble as though being tossed about to the left)* To the right… *(Everyone stumbles to the right)* Up… *(Everyone stumbles backwards)* Duck! *(Everyone stumbles forwards)*

Grandma: Here, this reminds me of a song. *(She sings)* 'You put your left arm in, your right arm out; in, out, in, out, you shake it all about. You do the hokey cokey and you turn around; that's what it's all about.'

Rick: *(Shouting anxiously)* It's no good, Computer, they're still gaining on us. I can see a black hole up ahead. I'm going in there to hide.

Computer: No, no, Rick! Stay away from the black hole. Steer round it!

Rick: It's too late, we're being sucked in!

Everyone starts to move around in slow motion, as if they are floating. They are not being tossed around any more.

Grandma: (Speaking slowly) Aaaahh! … My…teeth…are… coming… out.

Wendy: Hold… on…Grandma.

Computer: (Speech slowing down) We're… getting… sucked…in… I'm… fading… away!

Mummy: Where…are… we?

Wendy: We're… in… a… black… hole.

Mummy: That's… nice… dear!

Rick: (Looking horrified) The… computer… has… crashed… We've… lost… him.

Grandma: Oh… no… He… was… such… a… nice… chip… I… mean… chap…

Mummy: He… thought… we… were… special!

Wendy: He… chose… us…

Grandma: Even… Rick…

Mummy: Perhaps… he… needs… dusting… (She dusts his screen)

Computer: *(Voice back to normal)* Ha, ha! That tickles!

Rick: Who said that?

Computer: I did.

Grandma: What's going on?

Computer: Booting up. Booting up.

All: He's alive! Hooray!

Computer: We're coming out of the black hole. Your piloting must have been really slick, Rick!

Mummy: He might think you're slick, Rick, but your piloting has made me feel really sick, Rick!

Computer: Well, Rick's got us out of a fix. We're through the black hole. But now, I'm afraid, we're lost in space.

Grandma: I was lost at the seaside, once.

Computer: Shhh! I'm trying to finish off today's episode! *(He pauses and then says grandly)* Will we ever be found? What has happened to the Tarragons? Will Grandma ever know what's going on? Find out in the next exciting episode of… the Watt family!

Play the Watt family theme tune as actors exit.

Day Four: Breakthrough!

Computer: Space… it's really big out there! We made it through the black hole safe and sound—new planets to explore, new adventures lie ahead.

Grandma: I'm just going out for a walk. I could do with some fresh air.

Mummy: Yes, I think I'll clean the outside of the spaceship.

Rick: Yeah, I'm just nipping down the park for a game of football.

Wendy: And I'm going shopping.

Computer: Ahem! I don't think that's such a good idea.

All: Why not?

Computer: Grandma, there's no fresh air out there. In fact, there's no air, full stop.

Grandma: Oh dear, I thought I felt a bit breathless.

Computer: Mummy, if you clean the outside of the ship, you'll float away into outer space.

Mummy: I'm sure I'll find lots to clean out there.

Computer: Rick, there's no park or football.

Rick: What? Don't aliens know how to play football?

Reproduced with permission from *The Starship Discovery Holiday Club!* published by BRF 2008 (978 1 84101 545 3)

Computer:	Wendy, there are no shops in outer space.
Wendy:	No shops? Not even *[mention local shop]*?
All:	*(They begin to sob)* We want to go home.
Computer:	I'm sorry, I never said it was going to be easy, but I am here to guide you. We have many exciting places to visit.
Wendy:	*(Looking off stage, pretending to look out of the window)* Oh yes, I can see lots of lovely planets out of the window—and we have neighbours.
Grandma:	Neighbours? Oh yes, another spaceship.
Computer:	Red alert! Red alert! It's the Tarragon ship! They have made it through the black hole, too. Quick, Rick, you need to be slick, Rick, if we are to escape. You need to pilot this ship like Luke Skywalker!
Rick:	Who?

Rick, who is sitting down with the joystick controller, steers frantically, making revving engine noises. The others are standing up and overbalance as the space ship accelerates.

Computer:	Follow my instructions, Rick. It's going to take some ducking and diving. Ready? To the left… *(All the cast lean and stumble as though being tossed about to the left)* To the right… *(Everyone stumbles to the right)* Up… *(Everyone stumbles backwards)* Duck! *(Everyone stumbles forwards)* It's no use—we can't outrun them. We need to save fuel. Rick, slow down! *(The teleport starts to make a noise and fill with smoke)* The Tarragons are beaming aboard.

A big alien Tarragon steps out of the teleport. The Watt family panics and starts to run. Play some 'chase' music. The Tarragon chases Rick in a figure of eight, but runs into Grandma. They both fall over. The Tarragon and Grandma get up and he chases her for a bit. Wendy gets in the way so he chases Wendy, who suddenly stops and points up. The Tarragon looks up and Wendy hides. The Tarragon chases Mummy Watt. Suddenly, all actors freeze.

Computer:	Are the Tarragons trying to take over the spaceship? Is this life, but not as we know it? Find out in the next exciting episode of… the Watt family!

Play the Watt family theme tune as actors exit.

Day Five: Battle stations!

Computer:	Space… it's big out there! But it's tiny in here, especially now we've been joined by an alien Tarragon. He's been chasing the Watt family for hours.

The Watt family and the Tarragon are all leaning forward with their hands on their legs, panting hard and out of breath.

Tarragon:	*(Panting and out of breath)* I'm s-o-r-r-y for not wanting to send back your Mummy. It's just that she is such a good cleaner and her shepherd's pie was yummy—even though we all felt sorry for the shepherd. We wanted to keep her, but we know that was very selfish. Please forgive us.
Mummy:	Oh hello, Herbert, it's you.
Grandma:	What? *(To Mummy Watt)* You know him?
Mummy:	Oh yes, that's little Herbert. He's a lovely alien. *(To Herbert)* Now, dear, you're not to worry about the shepherd—you're not eating a shepherd, it's just the name of the pie.
Computer:	*(To the Tarragon)* Why have you beamed aboard our spaceship?
Tarragon:	Oh, I just wondered if Rick wanted to come and have a game of football aboard our ship.
Rick:	Football!
Tarragon:	And, Wendy, we have lots of wonderful shops on board.
Wendy:	Shops!
Tarragon:	We also have some lovely tea shops, Grandma. Our ship is huge—more like a small town, really. There's plenty to clean, Mummy Watt.
Wendy / Grandma:	Sounds wonderful.
Tarragon:	The truth is, we actually need your help. That's why we didn't want to let Mummy Watt go.
Computer:	Well, to tell you the truth, we need yours, too.
Tarragon:	Are you thinking what I'm thinking?
Computer:	Yes—neither ship is powerful enough to get back through the black hole.
Tarragon:	But if we work together and link the two ships up…
Computer:	With a tractor beam, the combined power will give us enough of a boost to get both ships back through the black hole.
Tarragon:	Exactly! I'll go back to my ship and let the crew know what we are going to do.

The Tarragon goes back into the teleport and disappears in a puff of smoke.

Computer: Tarragon ship tractor beam in place. Full speed ahead, Rick! *(Everyone starts to shake as Rick flies the ship. Play sound effect of the roar of an engine)* It's working! Both ships are able to get through the black hole. *(Everyone shakes even more)* We're almost there, Rick. *(Pause)* We're there! We've made it!

Wendy: *(Her mobile phone rings)* Oh, hello, Herbert Tarragon! What? Out with you tonight? Yes, please!

Computer: Could this be the start of a wonderful relationship with the Tarragons? Will Wendy ever get off the phone to her new Tarragon friend? We really must go. We have new places to see— who knows what is on the horizon? We hope you have enjoyed this adventure with the Watt family. Join us again soon for another amazing adventure with Grandma and Mummy, Rick and Wendy Watt!

Play the Watt family theme tune as actors exit.

Starship Discovery! crafts

Backpack oxygen bottles

Strap the two bottles together with masking tape. Cut strips of fabric to make straps that fit over the child's shoulders. Write words on separate labels: oxygen, food, water, Jesus, Bible, prayer and so on. Turn the bottles upside down so that the bottom is uppermost, and stick the labels at random on to the bottles. Make 'flames' with the crêpe paper and affix to the necks of the bottles with sticky tape. Fix the straps to the bottles with elastic bands.

Kaleidoscopes

Score the mirror-board from top to bottom down its length to make four equal sections, each measuring 4cm wide. Fold the mirror-board into a triangular prism, overlapping two sections at the bottom and holding them in place with sticky tape. Cover one end of the triangular prism with clingfilm and fix into position with sticky tape.

Place four translucent sequins on to the clingfilm and cover with greaseproof or tracing paper.

Cut a triangle of card measuring 4cm x 4cm x 4cm and cover it with black sugar paper. Punch a hole in the centre of the triangle and fix the triangle to the open end of the triangular prism using sticky tape. Cover the outside of the kaleidoscope with black sugar paper. As the kaleidoscope is turned, the patterns will change.

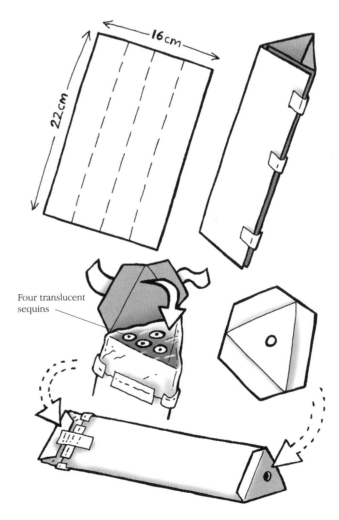

Four translucent sequins

33

Memory verse rockets

For each child, you will need:
One small cardboard tube, strong card, felt-tipped pens, aluminium cooking foil, plain sticky labels, PVA glue, stapler and sticky tape.

Cut four slits at equal distances around the base of the cardboard tube. Cut 'rocket fins' out of strong card, shaped as in the illustration below. Cut slits in the rocket fins as indicated. Interlock the fins and slip them on to the cardboard rocket tube.

Cut a circle of card measuring 5cm radius. Cut a triangular wedge out of the circle and shape the card into a cone shape to fit over the top of the rocket tube. Affix the cone to the top of the rocket with either PVA glue or sticky tape. Cover the whole rocket with aluminium foil. Write or copy the memory verses for each day on the sticky labels and stick them on to the rocket fins (for a template, see page 69).

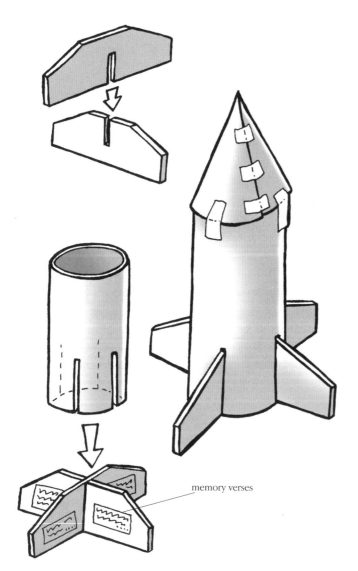

memory verses

Breakthrough spinners

For each child, you will need:
Two strong card circles, each measuring 15cm diameter, felt-tipped pens, PVA glue and a pencil.

Draw a picture of Jesus' disciple, Peter, on one of the card circles, placing him off centre to the left. Draw a picture of Jesus on the other card circle, also placing him off centre to the left. Colour in both pictures, giving them a dark background with lighter characters. Glue the two circles together (pictures on the outside), sandwiching the top of the pencil between them. Spin the pencil between your hands. The characters will look as if they are together.

Salt dough stars

For the salt dough you will need:
Four cups of plain flour, four cups of salt, and water to mix.

For each child, you will need:
One quantity of salt dough, a small rolling-pin, a star-shaped cutter, greaseproof paper, acrylic paints, a small paintbrush and buttonhole thread.

Mix the flour and salt together in a bowl and add enough water to make a soft dough. Roll the dough flat and cut out star shapes. Make a small hole in the top of one of the star's points. Place the dough star on greaseproof paper and bake in an oven at a low temperature until it has hardened. Allow to cool and paint the star. Thread buttonhole thread through the hole to form a loop for hanging.

Starship pictures

For each child, you will need:
One paper plate, white cartridge paper, a ribbon, felt-tipped pens, PVA glue and sticky tape.

Photocopy or trace the starship picture on page 35 on to the cartridge paper. Cut the paper into a circle to match the circle in the centre of the paper plate. Colour in the picture. Decorate the fluted edge of the plate with shooting stars, planets and other outer space images. Stick the picture in the middle of the paper plate, and fix a loop of ribbon to the back of the plate with sticky tape to form a hanger.

Outer space frieze

You will need:
Rolls of lining wallpaper (unpasted) or large sheets of card, collage scraps (fabric, shiny paper, corrugated cardboard, small plastic containers and so on), felt-tipped pens or poster paints, paintbrushes and PVA glue.

Use paint and collage materials to illustrate the theme for each day. Build the frieze day by day throughout the holiday club week. Display the frieze on the walls of your holiday club venue so that the children can see it building up as the holiday club progresses.

Starship Discovery! games

Starship Discovery relay races

Relay races are always popular. Depending on your budget, take some time to hunt out items in toy shops, catalogues and on the Internet to make the races more fun and 'spacey'!

Space hopper race

A space hopper is, of course, a big soft ball with handles that children can sit and bounce on. Often, you can buy them in sets of three at a reasonable price.

Line the children up in their teams, ready to race against the other teams. Give each team a space hopper. On the command 'Ready, steady, go', the first child has to bounce down the playing area, negotiating an obstacle course made from cones. When they get to the end of the course, they run back with the space hopper and give it to the next person in their team line. Continue until everyone in the team has had a turn. The winning team is the one to finish first.

Flying saucer race

Each team will need a flying saucer (Frisbee), four cones (markers) and a hoop.

Position each team's cones at set distances down the course—for example, between two and four metres apart. Position a leader at the end of each team's line of cones. The leader needs to be holding the hoop.

Four children in each team go and stand by a cone, one child at each cone. Of the remaining children, the first in line should be given the Frisbee. On the command 'Ready, steady, go!' that child throws the Frisbee to their teammate on the first marker, who throws it to the person on the second marker and so on down the course. The child at the last marker tries to throw the Frisbee through the hoop, which the leader is holding. The leader counts how many times the Frisbee goes through the hoop.

The child on the last marker runs and collects the Frisbee, whether or not it has gone through the hoop, and then runs to the front of their team line. As this child is running, the other children move so that the child at the first cone moves to the second cone and so on. The child with the Frisbee passes it to the new front-of-line child and proceeds to the back of the line. The new Frisbee holder throws it to their teammate on the first cone and the game continues until everyone has had a turn. The winning team is the one to get the most Frisbees through the hoop, rather than the team that finishes first.

Flying planet volleyball

You will need an inflatable globe. Alternatively, you could use a beach ball or balloon. Inflatable globes can be purchased from toy shops or ordered via the Internet.

Have two teams facing each other and two leaders holding a net or rope line between the teams. Explain that planet earth is always moving. In fact, all the planets in our solar system constantly orbit the sun. Play a game of planet volleyball. The game is played just like normal volleyball, in that the children have to knock the inflatable globe across the net, each team keeping the ball up in the air and knocking it back across the net. Teammates can knock it to one another before knocking it back, but they are not allowed to hold on to it. If the ball hits the floor, the team on the other side of the net scores a point.

Play the game for a set time. The team with the most points at the end of the playing time wins the game. For a fast and furious game, try adding more than one ball.

Space race

Have a relay race that includes all the above: space hoppers, flying saucers (Frisbees) and inflatable globes.

Line the children up in their teams. Place two cones apart, equally spaced, with the first two children each standing by a cone. Have the Frisbee by the first cone, ready to be thrown to the child at the second cone. Of the remaining children, the first in line should be given the inflatable globe.

On the command 'Ready, steady, go!' the child with the globe throws it to the child on the first cone, who throws the Frisbee to the child on the second cone. This child then jumps on to the space hopper, bounces to the finish line and runs to the back of the main line of children. All the children move forward one position, the first child in the main line moving to the first cone, the child on first cone moving to the second cone, and so on. Leaders need to move the equipment back into position, ready for the next child. The race continues until all the children in each team have had a turn at each position. The first team to finish is the winning team.

Red Dwarf

Split the group into equal teams. Place a chair for each team at the far end of the playing area. Holding on to their ankles, each team member must move up the hall, around the chair and back to their team, and tag the next person to go. The team that finishes first wins the game.

Crashing comets!

Split the group into teams of equal numbers. Instruct each team to sit in a circle, and place a basket or bucket in the middle of each team's circle. In the middle of the playing area, set a pile of eight balls or beanbags (more if you have more than four teams). Number each child in each team, starting at number one and continuing until all the children have a number.

Call out a number. All the children with that number have to dash to the middle of the playing area and grab *just one* 'comet' (ball or beanbag). They take the comet back to their team's circle and drop it into the basket or bucket. They continue running to the middle and grabbing a comet from the central pile until all the balls have gone. Once this has happened, they are then allowed to steal comets out of the other teams' buckets. The rest of the team are not allowed to stop them, but, of course, at the same time other children are taking *their* comets.

As soon as a child collects four comets for their team, their team leader must shout 'Crashing comets' to win the round. Continue playing until all the children have had a turn. The team that wins the most rounds wins the race.

Star gazers

Designate a corner of the room as a black hole. Choose a leader to be the red dwarf and occupy the black hole. The caller calls out the following commands to the children, who respond as described:

- Shooting stars: Run around the room.
- Star dusters: Pretend to dust the room.
- Starfish: Pretend to fish.
- Star turn: Spin round.
- Superstars: Wave your hands.
- Starbursts: Jump up and down.
- Red dwarf: The red dwarf comes out of the black hole to catch a star gazer and takes them back to the black hole, where they must stay until the end of the game. The last star gazer to be caught wins the game.

Meteorites

You will need a pack of dried peas, drinking straws and two saucers. Split the groups into teams of three or four. Each team stands in a line. Place a saucer of dried peas (meteorites) on the floor in front of each team line, and give each team member a straw. Each person must take it in turn to suck a pea on to the end of the straw and run with it to the other saucer, which has been placed at the other end of the playing area. The team that transfers the most meteorites in a limited time wins the game.

Star clusters

The group dances around the room to music. When the music stops, the leader shouts out a number (such as 'four'). Everyone has to form a group of that number. Those who don't manage to form the right numbered group are out of the game. The winners are the children left in the game at the end of a designated playing time.

Star attraction

Half the group sit on chairs in a circle, facing inwards. The other half of the group stand behind those sitting on the chairs. Leave one chair empty, but have someone standing behind it. The person standing behind the empty chair invites one of the sitters (stars) to come and sit in that chair by winking at them. The sitter who was winked at must try to get up and escape to the empty chair before the person standing behind their own chair can stop them by placing his or her hands on their shoulders. If the sitter succeeds in getting away, the person standing behind the now empty chair tries to attract another 'star' by winking at them. The game continues for a defined length of time. If desired, half way through the playing time, the players can change places so that the sitters become the standers and vice versa.

Jumping Jupiter

Have the children standing on one side of the room. A leader shouts out the name of a colour, followed by 'jumping Jupiter'—for example, 'Red jumping Jupiter'. All the children wearing red have to try to jump across to the other side of the room, while a jumping leader tries to tag them. When a child is caught, they join the jumping leader in the middle and can jump to try to tag other jumping Jupiters. The jumping Jupiter to survive the longest is the winner.

Puppet sketches

Day One: Blast off!

Turning

God doesn't force us to do anything, but longs for us to turn to him and make the right choice.

Lucy:	Bert, what do you want to do this afternoon?
Bert:	I don't know. What do you want to do?
Lucy:	I asked you first. What do you want to do?
Bert:	The same as you.
Lucy:	Great—and what's that?
Bert:	I don't know…?
Lucy:	Oh, Bert!
Bert:	Let's have a game of football.
Lucy:	Great, let's! Where?
Bert:	Just outside my house—there, in the road— and there's a big wall by the railway line. We could kick the ball against that.
Lucy:	I'm not sure about that. We could go to the park.
Bert:	I suppose, but the park's about 15 minutes' walk away.
Lucy:	That's all right. We'll pass Gordon Bennett and Shaz on the way. We could see if they wanted to play, too.
Bert:	Yeah, but I like kicking the ball against the wall, and there's no wall at the park.
Lucy:	No, just a huge field, with loads of space for kicking the ball!
Bert:	I suppose, but…
Lucy:	It's dangerous kicking a ball in the road next to a railway line—but it's your choice.
Bert:	Why?
Lucy:	'Cos it's your ball.
Bert:	I've had a great idea!
Lucy:	What's that, then?
Bert:	We could go to the park and have a game of football and see if Gordon Bennett and Shaz want to come, too.
Lucy:	The right choice, Bert! Say goodbye, then!
Bert:	Goodbye, then!
Lucy:	Bye!

Day Two: Beam me up!

Trusting

God will be there for us.

Bert:	Lucy, Lucy, how do you fancy coming for a swim later on?
Lucy:	Er… well… er…
Bert:	Go on, it'll be cool!
Lucy:	Er… no, thanks.
Bert:	Oh, go on, Lucy, it'll be more fun with two.
Lucy:	I can't.
Bert:	Why not?
Lucy:	I've got to go and er… um… walk the budgie.
Bert:	Walk the budgie?
Lucy:	No, er… hoover the lawn.
Bert:	Hoover the lawn? Lucy, you're making excuses. Just say 'yes'!
Lucy:	Yes!
Bert:	G-r-e-a-t!
Lucy:	I mean, No!
Bert:	No? Why not?
Lucy:	I just don't want to.
Bert:	But why?
Lucy:	Because…
Bert:	Because what?
Lucy:	Don't tell anyone, but… (She whispers in his ear)
Bert:	(He blurts it out) You can't swim!

Reproduced with permission from *The Starship Discovery Holiday Club!* published by BRF 2008 (978 1 84101 545 3)

Lucy:	Bert, I told you not to tell anyone.
Bert:	I didn't.
Lucy:	Well, apart from this lot… *(Looking at audience)*
Bert:	Oh yeah! Sorry, but why didn't you say so?
Lucy:	Because I didn't want everyone to know, that's why.
Bert:	Why not?
Lucy:	Because I'm the only person in the whole world who can't swim, and it's embarrassing, that's why.
Bert:	But there are lots of people who can't swim, and it's not embarrassing. I couldn't swim once.
Lucy:	You, Bert? I thought you could do everything.
Bert:	Not everything, just most things. Look, Lucy, I swim like a fish. I'll teach you.
Lucy:	I swim like a stone—straight down! *(She looks at Bert)* Would you really teach me?
Bert:	It would be an honour to teach you.
Lucy:	No messing about?
Bert:	No, Lucy, you can trust me. Learning to swim is a serious business. So are you going to come?
Lucy:	If you promise I won't get wet!
Bert:	Er…?
Lucy:	Only joking! Of course I'll come, as long as it's not raining. I don't want to get wet.
Bert:	You've cracked that joke already.
Lucy:	Oh yeah! Let's go, then, Bert! Bye, everyone!
Bert:	Bye!

Day Three: Black hole!

Tripping

God forgives us when we let him down.

Bert:	*(Comes up, but Lucy doesn't)* Come on, Lucy, you're late… again.
Lucy:	Sorry, but I've painted a picture that I wanted to bring to show all the children. I left it on the table at home, ready to bring this morning. Have you seen it?
Bert:	On the table, you say?
Lucy:	Yeah! *(She appears, looking fed up)*
Bert:	Did it have a picture on it?
Lucy:	I just said it did.
Bert:	It wasn't a painting of what could be described as a spaceship, was it?
Lucy:	Yes.
Bert:	With aliens waving out of the window?
Lucy:	Yes! So you have seen it.
Bert:	No! Whatever gave you that idea?
Lucy:	Yes, you have! Stop messing me about!

	Where is it?
Bert:	It's… er… gone.
Lucy:	I know it's gone. *(Staring right at Bert)* What have you done with it?
Bert:	I know! Rather than showing everyone your picture, let's describe it and let them use their imaginations. It's good to use your imagination.
Lucy:	Bert, you're scaring me now. What have you done?
Bert:	I'm sorry, Lucy. I was desperate to make a paper aeroplane, but I couldn't find any paper. Then I saw your picture and it was just the right size, so I turned it into a paper aeroplane.
Lucy:	So my alien spaceship is now a paper aeroplane?
Bert:	Er… *was* a paper aeroplane…
Lucy:	Was?
Bert:	Er… yes. It flew very well, straight out the window and into the road, where it was squashed by a lorry. Therefore, your alien spaceship that was changed into a paper aeroplane is no more.
Lucy:	*(Stunned)* I'm stunned, Bert! You're normally such a sensible lad. You've let me down big-time. I was very proud of my picture.
Bert:	I'm really, really, really, really sorry. I know! You can have one of my sweets.

Lucy still looks upset and doesn't say a word.

Bert:	Two of my sweets?

Lucy still looks upset.

Bert:	A bar of chocolate!
Lucy:	Getting closer.
Bert:	OK, Lucy, I'll buy a bar of chocolate for us to share while we make a spaceship out of plastic bottles. We can make playdough aliens and everything.
Lucy:	OK, you're forgiven. Let's go!
Bert:	Phew! Bye, everyone!

Day Four: Breakthrough!

Transforming

It makes all the difference when your God is with you.

Bert: *(He comes up without Lucy)* Oh no, where is she this time? *(Lucy snores out of sight. Bert looks below)* Ha! She's gone to sleep! Let's wake her… after three. We'll shout, 'Wake up, Lucy!' Are you ready? One, two, three… WAKE UP, LUCY!

Lucy: Aaaaaaaaaaghhhhhhh! *(She comes up very worried and looking around)* Where is he, Bert?

Bert: What? Who?

Lucy: What do you mean, what, who?

Bert: Lucy, I don't know what you're talking about.

Lucy: The dog the size of an elephant.

Bert: What dog the size of an elephant?

Lucy: The one that's chasing me.

Bert: There's no dog the size of an elephant chasing you.

Lucy: I bet he's behind me, isn't he? *(She turns round slowly)*

Bert: Ruff! Ruff!

Lucy: Aaaaaaaaaaaghhhhh! *(She turns back quickly)* Did you hear him, Bert?

Bert: Sorry, Lucy, but that was me. I couldn't resist it. Who let the dog out? Who! Who! Who! Who!

Lucy: I didn't. He climbed out after me through the letterbox.

Bert: Lucy, there isn't a dog. It was me! It just reminded me of that song: 'Who let the dogs out?'

Lucy: *(Not listening)* I know he's here somewhere.

Bert: Lucy, you're barking mad! Ha! Do you get it? Barking mad! Hang on, did you say a dog the size of an elephant climbed through the letterbox?

Lucy: Yeah, he's after me.

Bert: Lucy, it must have been a dream, because a dogs the size of an elephant can't climb through a letterbox.

Lucy: *(She calms down)* Oh yeah! But it all seemed so real. I dreamt I was doing my paper round. When I came to number 46, I pushed a paper through and heard a bark. Then this dog the size of an elephant jumped through the letterbox and started chasing me.

Bert: Well, you don't have to be scared any more, now you know that it's just a dream.

Lucy: But I am, Bert. I have to do my paper round tomorrow and they do have a dog at number 46. What if it jumps through the letterbox again?

Bert: It won't.

Lucy: It might! *(She starts to shake)*

Bert: Cor, Lucy! You really are scared, aren't you? I'm going to regret saying this, but… Lucy, would it help if I came with you?

Lucy: Oh yeah! It will make all the difference to know that big, brave Bert is right there with me.

Bert: OK, I'll come. What time do you leave the house in the morning?

Lucy: Six o'clock.

Bert: What?

Lucy: You promised.

Bert: Yeah, tomorrow I'll come with you.

Lucy: G-r-e-a-t! Bye, everyone!

Bert: Bye!

Day Five: Battle station!

Training

God always hears us when we call to him.

Bert: *(To Lucy)* I don't suppose you have time to listen, either.

Lucy: Of course I have. What's up?

Bert: You have? Really?

Lucy: Yeah!

Bert: Yeah, but I don't suppose you're really interested, are you?

Lucy: Of course I am, Bert. You're my mate.

Bert: Oh, wow! I've got some great news! I've been invited along to an audition to sing in a new pop group, similar to Pop Idol.

Lucy: Wow! Bert, that's really exciting! I'm surprised you seem so down about it. What's up?

Bert: Well, it's such great news, I had to tell someone, so I thought—who can I phone to tell the good news? I know, I thought, I'll tell… *(he names a current female pop singer)* I love her music, so she's bound to be interested to know I'm going to be a pop star like her.

Lucy: Wow, you phoned… *(she names the singer)* What did she say?

Bert: Nothing. I tried and tried and tried to find her telephone number, but couldn't. I went online to send an email, but she never replied.

Lucy: Shame! But I'm not surprised. She must have thousands of people trying to speak to her every day. She couldn't possibly speak to them all.

Bert: Yeah, I suppose you're right. So then I tried

Lucy: to tell Mum, but she was on the phone to someone. In fact, she's probably still on the phone, and that was yesterday.

Lucy: Knowing your mum, you're probably right.

Bert: So then I tried to tell Dad, but he was cutting the lawn and it was hard to make myself heard. He was nodding away, but I could tell he wasn't listening. I could have said anything and he'd still have been nodding away.

Lucy: Well, yes, it's hard to have a conversation and cut the grass at the same time.

Bert: Then I tried to tell my brother, but he was playing a computer game at the time and, once again, he wasn't interested. You're the first person I've managed to tell.

Lucy: What was that? Sorry, I wasn't listening!

Bert: What?

Lucy: Only joking! It's great news. Well done, Bert. Can I hear what you're going to sing?

Bert sings a song.

Lucy: Bert, you have a unique voice. Bye, everyone!

Bert: Thanks, Lucy… I think! Yeah, bye, everyone!

Quick quiz questions

Quizzes are a wonderful way of recapping what the children have learnt and a good opportunity for the children to earn points for their team. Some of the quick quiz questions below are about the Bible story and Bible memory verses, some are about the Watt family and some are general knowledge and just for fun. The questions are age-banded as follows:

- Question 1 is for the youngest group.
- Question 2 is for the middle group.
- Question 3 is for the oldest group.

Bible story and memory verse

1. In today's Bible story, what was the name of Jesus' friend?
   (Peter)
2. Where in the Bible can today's memory verse be found?
   (Joshua 24:15)
3. What does it say?
   (Choose yourself today whom you will serve; as for me, I will serve the Lord.)

Day One: Blast off!

General knowledge

1. What is the name of our planet?
   (Earth)
2. Which one is the odd one out: Earth, Mars, Banana or Venus?
   (Banana)
3. What is the name of the spacecraft that goes into and out of space?
   (The space shuttle)

The Watt family

1. What is the name of the boy in the Watt family drama?
   (Rick)
2. What is the name of the girl in the Watt family drama?
   (Wendy)
3. For what special assignment have the Watt family been chosen?
   (To explore space)

Day Two: Beam me up!

The Watt family

1. What happened to Mummy Watt in yesterday's drama?
   (She was transported away)
2. What is the name of the space aliens?
   (The Tarragons)
3. What was the computer's rescue plan?
   (To swap Mummy Watt with a mop made to look like Grandma Watt)

Bible story and memory verses

1. What was Peter's job in yesterday's Bible story?
   (He was a fisherman)
2. What was yesterday's Bible verse?
   (Joshua 24:15)
3. What is today's Bible verse?
   (Proverbs 3:5)

Bible story

1. What did the fishermen catch after they had fished all night?
   (Nothing)
2. Why did Jesus want to borrow Peter's boat?
   (So that he could speak to the crowd)
3. After Jesus had helped the fishermen to catch loads of fish, what did he say they would do then?
   (Catch people instead of fish)

Day Three: Black hole!

The Watt family

1. In the Watt family drama, were the Tarragons happy with the mop?
   (No!)
2. Where did Rick try to hide to escape from the Tarragon spaceship?
   (In a black hole)
3. What happened to the computer?
   (It crashed)

Bible memory verses

1. As a team, sing the Bible memory verse from Day One.
   (Choose yourself today whom you will serve; as for me, I will serve the Lord)
2. As a team, sing yesterday's Bible memory verse.
   (Trust in the Lord with all your heart, and lean not on your own understanding)
3. As a team, finish today's Bible memory verse: 'Christ Jesus…
   (… came into the world to save sinners)

Bible story

1. Where were the disciples when Jesus, amazingly, started to walk towards them?
   (In a boat)
2. When the disciples first saw Jesus walking towards them, what did they think he was?
   (A ghost)
3. Peter also walked on the water, but why did he sink?
   (Because he was scared and stopped trusting Jesus)

Day Four: Breakthrough!

The Watt family

1. In the Watt family drama, what did Grandma Watt want to do when she grew bored of being in space?
   (Go for a walk)
2. Who besides the Watt family made it through the black hole?
   (The Tarragons)
3. What made the Watt family really scared?
   (The Tarragons beaming aboard the Starship Discovery)

Bible memory verses

1. As a team, sing any of the Bible memory verses you have learnt so far.
2. As a team, sing another Bible memory verse that you have learnt.
3. As a team, sing another Bible memory verse.

Bible story

1. What did Peter promise Jesus he would never do?
   (Run away)
2. How many times did Peter say he didn't know Jesus?
   (Three times)
3. After Peter denied knowing Jesus, what did he do?
   (He ran away and cried bitterly)

Day Five: Battle stations!

The Watt family

1. In the Watt family drama, is the Tarragon nasty or nice?
   (Nice)
2. What is the name of the Tarragon?
   (Herbert)
3. How did the Tarragons and the Watt family help each other?
   (They shared power to enable their spaceships to get back through the black hole)

Bible memory verses

1. As a team, sing any of the Bible memory verses you have learnt so far.
2. As a team, sing another Bible memory verse that you have learnt.
3. As a team, sing another Bible memory verse.

Bible story

1. Why were Peter and the other disciples so sad?
   (Because Jesus had been killed)
2. What made them happy again?
   (They found out that Jesus had risen from the tomb)
3. Whose arrival was heralded by a strong wind and what looked like tongues of fire? What difference did he make to the disciples?
   (The Holy Spirit; he made them brave)

Bible story narrations

Day One: Blast off!

Turning

Read Matthew 4:18–22, Mark 1:16–20 and Luke 5:1–11.

Today we hear how Peter chose to turn away from his old life to follow Jesus.

In Luke's account of the story, Jesus asks Peter to let the fishing nets down into the water. Peter obeys Jesus, even though he may not have agreed with him. Obedience brings results! It is very likely that Peter knew of Jesus already, but this is the first time that Jesus asks Peter to turn to him and make a choice—the choice to follow Jesus. Peter doesn't stop to weigh up the pros and cons of following Jesus: his choice is willing and immediate.

Peter's choice is costly: it means giving up all that he knows and holds dear. Matthew and Mark both record that Peter immediately dropped his nets and went with Jesus. He 'left' and 'followed'. His decision was followed up by action. In the same way, Christians today need to follow up their decision to turn to Jesus with action. They need to 'believe' and 'follow'. When Jesus asked Peter to make the choice to follow him, it was not just to have a passive role of listening and learning; it was to have an active role—to become someone who would 'catch people for God'. It marked a major turning point in Peter's life. Things would never be the same again.

> ### Cast
> Narrator, and two others (A and B) standing with their backs to the audience.

Narr: There was a man in the Bible who worked really hard—really, really hard. In fact, he often worked right through the night. He was a fisherman, and so were his friends.

A and B turn around together and pretend to fish with a fishing rod.

Narr: What are you doing?
A and B: Pretending to be fishermen.
Narr: No! They didn't have fishing rods like that. They had a fishing boat with fishing nets.
A and B: Oh! *(Both mime throwing nets overboard and struggling to pull in the nets)* Cor! Look at all those fish!
Narr: Wrong again! There weren't any fish that night. They fished all night, but caught nothing!
A and B: *(Looking fed up)* Here, fishy, fishy, fishy!

A and B keep miming throwing the nets overboard and pulling them in, looking hopeful, then disappointed.

Narr: You won't catch anything like that. I've already said, 'They fished all night, but caught nothing!' It wasn't always like that, though. Sometimes they caught boatloads of fish, but not tonight.

A and B continue to look fed up and shrug their shoulders.

A: May as well go home, then.
B: Yeah.
Narr: You can't just go home! You need to remember that you're in a boat in the middle of the lake.
A and B: Oh yeah!

Narr:	Anyway, you've now worked right through the night. It's morning. You row the boat to the shore and sit down to clean and mend any broken nets.
A:	Cor, this is hard work! But I love it!
B:	Yeah, I wouldn't want to do anything else. Sometimes we catch l-o-a-d-s of fish.
Narr:	Suddenly you notice someone walking along the seashore…
A:	Here, I've just noticed someone walking along the seashore.
Narr:	… and he's being followed by a huge crowd of people.
B:	Look! He's being followed by a huge crowd of people!
Narr:	The man saw the fisherman and got in to their boat.
A:	Here, he's got into our boat.
Narr:	They recognized him straight away, it was… *(said with excitement)* JESUS!
B:	Here, I recognize him! It's… *(said with equal excitement)* JESUS!
Narr:	Jesus asked the fishermen if he could borrow their boat.
A:	Err! Jesus we fished all night and caught nothing.
B:	But seeing it's you…
Narr:	But Jesus didn't seem to want to go fishing—well, not straight away. He wanted to use the boat as a platform, somewhere he could sit so that everyone could hear him. So all the crowd sat down on the seashore and Jesus sat down in the boat, and he started to speak to them. Sometimes he was funny…
A:	Oh, that's really very funny!
Narr:	… and sometimes he was serious.
B:	Oh, that's really very serious!
Narr:	Eventually, Jesus sent the crowd home. Then he said to the fishermen, 'Let's go fishing!'
A:	Err! Jesus, we fished all night and caught nothing. But seeing it's you, we'll go fishing.
B:	*(Whispers loudly to A)* Here, what does Jesus do for a job?
A:	He's a carpenter.
B:	A carpenter? So he doesn't know anything about fishing, then?
Narr:	Then Jesus said, 'Let your nets down to catch some fish.'
A:	There won't be any fish here…
B:	… but seeing it's you…

A and B mime throwing over the nets. Then, to their surprise, they struggle to pull them in.

Narr:	Yes, you've guessed it! There were loads of fish—so many, in fact, that they struggled to pull them in. Then, suddenly, Simon Peter—

	who was one tough fisherman—fell on his knees in front of Jesus *(B mimes this)* and said…
B:	Lord, don't come near me! I am a sinner!
Narr:	Jesus said to Peter, 'Don't be afraid! From now on you will bring in people instead of fish.
A:	What? Jesus chose those guys to be part of his team?
Narr:	He sure did! They pulled their boats on to the beach. Then they left everything—even that huge catch of fish—and teamed up with Jesus.
B:	I don't blame them. I'd have done the same. You can't turn down an invitation like that.
Narr:	They started out on the adventure of a lifetime, and Jesus was with them every step of the way.

Day Two: Beam me up!

Trusting

Read Matthew 14:22–32.

Peter's attempt to copy Jesus is a vivid lesson about the role that faith plays when we follow Jesus. In this story, it is easy to identify with Peter's impulsive yet vulnerable personality. Peter doesn't attempt what is naturally impossible until he hears the command from Jesus. He obeys Jesus' call but loses faith when he allows fear and doubt to get in the way. However, the minute Peter feels his faith failing, he turns to Jesus for help—and Jesus is there for him.

> ### Cast
> Narrator and two others (A and B)

Narr:	Have you ever been out with your friends and had an excellent day? Have you noticed that, on the way home, you just have to talk about it?
A:	*(Excitedly)* Wow! What a day!
B:	Yeah, a truly excellent day!
Narr:	I'm sure this happened a lot in the Bible—especially when you hung around with Jesus. One day had been a particularly long day, but an amazingly exciting one. Jesus told his friends to get into the boat and he would meet them later across the other side of the lake. Jesus went off up a mountain to pray, so his disciples jumped into Peter's boat and off

Reproduced with permission from *The Starship Discovery Holiday Club!* published by BRF 2008 (978 1 84101 545 3)

they went. (*Whole cast mimes getting into a boat*) I wonder what they talked about?

A: Cor! What a day!

B: Yeah, an amazing day!

A: Cor! All those people—at least five thousand men, plus the women and children.

B: Yeah! And all that food.

A: Err! No food at all at first—well, apart from that little boy's lunch.

B: Oh yeah! Fantastic! Jesus fed all those people with just five small loaves and two fish—and there were twelve full baskets left over.

Narr: Here, do you mind not talking about food while we're on this boat, going up and down? It's all right for you fishermen, but I'm feeling a bit…

A: Look! He's turning green.

Narr: (*Turning his head to stage left*) Yeah, I must be ill, 'cos I thought I saw someone walking on the water over there.

A: What?

B: Don't be daft! (*A and B both turn to look and then look terrified*) Oh no! He's right!

A: (*Screams*) Aagh! It's a ghost walking on the water! Let's get out of here!

Narr: (*To audience*) But it wasn't a ghost! Suddenly they heard a voice saying, 'Don't worry! I am Jesus. Don't be afraid.'

A: Sounds like Jesus.

Narr: It is Jesus.

B: Walking on the water?

Narr: Walking on the water!

B: Wow!

Narr: … said Peter.

B: Lord, if it is really you, tell me to come to you on the water.

Narr: Jesus said, 'Come on!' So Peter got out of the boat and started walking towards Jesus. (*B mimes this in slow motion*) But, suddenly, Peter noticed the wind and the waves. He became frightened—in fact, very frightened—and started to sink.

B: (*Shouts*) Save me, Lord!

Narr: Jesus reached out his hand and helped Peter up. Together, they both climbed in to the boat. 'You don't have much faith,' said Jesus. 'Why did you doubt?' Peter fell to his knees!

B: (*Falls to his knees and speaks slowly with reverence*) You really are the Son of God!

Pause.

A: How daft! Fancy Peter sinking like that! He must have known Jesus would save him.

Narr: Perhaps, but don't forget that we know the end of the story, whereas Peter couldn't have known for sure what would happen—but at least he was prepared to put his faith in Jesus

in the first place.

B: Yeah! The other disciples just watched. It was Peter who took the step of faith.

Narr: Yes, and it was Peter who experienced God's saving power as Jesus reached out to him.

A: I suppose the others missed out.

Narr: So be like Peter: put your trust in Jesus!

A: We may get scared and fail from time to time…

B: But Jesus promises to be with us always.

Day Three: Black hole!

Tripping

Read Matthew 26:69–75; Mark 14:66–72; Luke 22:56–62; John 18:15–18 and 25–27.

When Peter denies Jesus, his rejection stands in sharp contrast to Jesus' bold declaration before the council of the religious authorities. As the questions continue to fly, Peter digs himself in deeper and deeper. We, too, are more liable to fail Jesus in the heat of the moment or the depth of our despair. But Jesus understands our humanity, and his compassion meets us in our hour of deepest remorse.

> ### Cast
> Narrator and two others (A and B).

Narr: It's easy to say one thing and then do another.

A: I did that once. Mum and Dad were going out and I said I would do all the washing up. And I meant it… I really, really meant it!

B: Did you do it?

A:: No! I forgot!

Narr: That happened to Peter.

A: What? He forgot to do the washing up?

Narr: No, silly, he said one thing and then did another.

A: Peter said Jesus was great.

B: The greatest!

Narr: He had realized that Jesus was the Son of God.

B: He said Jesus was great.

A: The greatest!

Narr: But Peter knew there was trouble ahead.

A: He knew that lots of people wanted Jesus out of the way.

B: They were jealous because Jesus was so popular.

Narr: They didn't realize that Jesus was the Son of God.

A: But Peter decided he would stand by Jesus. He would even die for him if he had to.

B: Even if all the others reject you, I never will!

Narr: But Jesus said to him, 'Peter, I promise you that before a cock crows tonight, you will say three times that you don't know me.'

A: Wow! That hurt!

B: Even if I have to die with you, I will never say that I don't know you!

A: And he meant it… he really meant it.

Narr: Soon after that, while Jesus was praying in the garden of Gethsemane, a crowd armed with swords and clubs came to arrest him.

B: Peter drew his sword and swung it viciously at the crowd.

A: But he was a fisherman, not a soldier!

B: Well, he had brought a sword along anyway, and he struck at the high priest's servant, cutting off his right ear. Ouch!

A: Jesus touched the servant's ear and healed him, and then he said…

Narr: Peter, put your sword away. Anyone who lives by fighting will die by fighting. I could have called more than twelve armies of angels to fight for me if I had wanted. But then, how could the words of the scriptures come true, which say that this must happen?

B: Then he said to those who had come to arrest him…

Narr: Why do you come with swords and clubs? I'm not a criminal.

A: Then they arrested Jesus. His disciples were terrified. They legged it—all, that is, apart from John and Peter.

B: Yeah, they were scared all right, but they wanted to be with Jesus. So they followed from a distance and went straight into the courtyard of the high priest's house.

A: *(Excitedly)* So if some big tough soldier had come along and challenged Peter, he would have been brave.

B: Yes, he certainly would! He would have put up a fight, all right.

A: But it didn't happen like that, did it?

B: No. Peter was warming himself by the fire…

A: … when suddenly a servant girl said…

Narr: Here! Aren't you one of Jesus' followers?

B: Err! What? *(Sounds surprised)* No, no! No, not me!

Narr: Yes, you are! You were with Jesus of Galilee.

B: No! You're mistaken.

A: No need to get all aggressive!

Narr: Of course you were with him! Your accent gives you away.

A: Peter became really angry and started to hotly deny that he knew Jesus.

B: I've never met the man. May God punish me if I'm telling a lie!

Narr: Just then, a cock crowed, and Jesus turned and looked straight at Peter.

A: Peter was devastated. Suddenly, he remembered what Jesus had said: 'Before a cock crows tomorrow morning you will say three times that you don't know me.' He went out and cried hard.

Narr: Yes, Peter thought he was a tough guy, but here he was in tears. He knew he had let down his best friend.

B: I told Jesus I was no good, a loser, and that I would only let him down, but he still asked me to follow him. If only I had said no, none of this would have happened. Oh, why did he choose me? I told him I was useless—but he still chose me!

Narr: God loves to use people who realize they are weak, people who know they can't do it on their own—people who realize they need God.

A: Later on, Jesus forgave Peter.

B: And Peter went on to speak up boldly for Jesus.

Narr: God knows we will make mistakes, but he longs to forgive us.

A and B: Because God loves us so much! *(Thumbs up)*

Day Four: Breakthrough!

Transforming

Read Acts 2:1–47.

Jesus' promises always come true. He will always help us speak boldly for him and he turns our weakness into strength.

> ### Cast
> Narrator and two others (A and B).

Narr: Have you ever had a friend…

A: … a best friend…

B: … who you do everything with—football, swimming, watching TV.

Narr: Then one day that friend says they're moving.

A: *(To B)* Moving? Where?

B: Dad's got a new job, and we've got to move.

A: You can't!

B: I've got to!

A: But… but… but… I don't want you to.

Reproduced with permission from *The Starship Discovery Holiday Club!* published by BRF 2008 (978 1 84101 545 3)

B: I don't want to, either, but I've got to.

Play sad music while A and B hug emotionally and then move four steps apart, looking sad, blowing their noses, wiping their eyes, waving and so on.

Narr: It's very hard when someone you love goes away.
A: You feel lonely.
B: What will you do without them?
Narr: That's what happened to Peter and the other disciples…
A: … after Jesus had died on the cross.
B: We felt lost without him.
Narr: But then he came back to life!
A and B: ALIVE! We're so happy!
Narr: But then he had to leave them again.
A and B: Oh no!
Narr: But Jesus promised to send someone to help them.
A: Someone to help them?
B: No one could ever take Jesus' place.
Narr: Someone who would give them strength; someone who would guide them.
A and B: WHO?
Narr: The Holy Spirit! He is God, just as Jesus is God. He will always be with you. He will help you and make you brave. He will guide you and give you power.
A: Erm… do you mean like a battery for a torch?
B: Don't be daft!
Narr: Well, yes, a bit like a battery for a torch. A torch without power is useless.
A: We feel so alone.
B: Who will protect us?
A: We really miss Jesus.
B: Yeah, we feel weak and scared. Let's hide!
Narr: So they shut themselves away all together in one house.
A: Suddenly…
B: *(Looking up and in a loud voice)* … there was a loud noise from the sky.
A: It sounded like a strong wind blowing through the house.
B: Then we saw what looked like tongues…
A: Tongues of fire!
B: They settled on each one of us.
Narr: The Holy Spirit had arrived in power, filling each person.
A: Suddenly…
B: … we weren't scared any more.
Narr: As Jesus had promised, the Holy Spirit had arrived in style.
A: We went out into the streets.
B: We told everyone the good news.
A: And everyone understood what we were saying…

B: … in their own language!
Narr: Three thousand people believed their message and became Christians.
A: And Peter, the one who thought he was a nobody, the one who denied Jesus and ran away…
B: … wasn't scared any more! In fact, he did most of the speaking and ended up becoming a leader of the church.
Narr: Jesus hadn't abandoned them. His Holy Spirit was now living inside them.
A and B: Thank you, Jesus!

Day Five: Battle stations!

Training

Read Acts 12:6–19.

When Peter was put in prison for speaking out boldly for Jesus, perhaps he didn't realize that Jesus was still beside him, even if Peter was not aware of the fact. Jesus rescues us in ways that are sometimes beyond our wildest dreams. Peter's rescue was backed by the disciples' prayers, and we, too, should pray with the expectation that God will answer. The story shows us that God answers our prayers for a purpose.

Cast
Narrator and two others (A and B).

Narr: *(To A)* Do you ever dream?
A: *(Excitedly)* Oh, yes! Sometimes I have really nice dreams and I'm really disappointed when I wake up. I try to go back to sleep again.
Narr: *(To B)* Do you ever dream?
B: Sometimes, but often I don't like my dreams. They scare me. When I have a nightmare, I'm relieved to wake up.
A: *(To Narrator)* Do you ever dream?
Narr: Oh, yes! But my dreams never seem to make sense. Sometimes I dream that my friends and I are chatting away to TV stars—but in the strangest of places.
A: Dreams can sometimes seem so real.
Narr: Once, a strange thing happened to Peter.
A: It was so strange that he wasn't sure whether he was dreaming or whether it was real.
B: Horrid King Herod Agrippa had had James, the brother of John, arrested and put to death.

Narr:	Now he had arrested Peter and thrown him in jail—intending to have him put to death too.
A:	The people of the church never stopped praying to God for Peter.
B:	He was chained between two guards…
A:	… and there were more guards on duty at the prison gate.
B:	There was no escape.
Narr:	Peter was fast asleep.
A:	Fast asleep? How could he sleep at a time like that?
B:	Perhaps he trusted God.

B sinks to the floor and pretends to sleep.

Narr:	Suddenly an angel of the Lord stood there, and a light shone in the cell. The angel shook Peter by the shoulder, woke him up and said…
A:	*(Shaking B by the shoulders)* Quick! Get up!
Narr:	At once the chains fell off Peter's hands.
A:	Get dressed and put on your sandals. *(B mimes this)* Now put on your coat and follow me.
Narr:	The angel led Peter out of the prison. Peter followed him, but he thought he was having a dream.
B:	Past the first guard…
A:	Didn't the guard wake up?
Narr:	No.
A:	Didn't he see Peter, then?
Narr:	Apparently not.
B:	Past the second guard…
A:	Tut tut! Not sleeping on duty, surely?
Narr:	Well, they were highly trained soldiers. They wouldn't sleep on duty, but…
B:	… And out through the iron gate leading to the city.
Narr:	Peter walked free, and found himself standing in the city street. Then the angel left him.
B:	Wow! Now I know that it is really true. The Lord sent his angel to rescue me from Herod's power.
Narr:	He went to the home of Mary, the mother of John Mark. Many people had gathered there and were praying.
B:	Knock, knock!
A:	Who's there?
B:	Peter.
A:	Peter who?
B:	Peter! Peter!
A:	Wow!
Narr:	The servant girl, Rhoda, ran back to the others. She was so excited, she forgot to open the door.
A:	It's Peter.
B:	Peter who?

A:	Peter! Peter!
B:	Are you mad? Peter's in prison. It must be his angel.
Narr:	Eventually they opened the door, and there was Peter! They were amazed to see him.
A:	How daft!
Narr:	What?
A:	Why were they so amazed that God had rescued Peter? Why wouldn't they believe it was him?
B:	Yeah, they had been praying all night that God would rescue him—and when he did, they didn't believe it.
Narr:	God really does hear our prayers, and he always answers them.
A:	Isn't it brilliant to know that God listens to us when we talk to him?
B:	It certainly is!

Reproduced with permission from *The Starship Discovery Holiday Club!* published by BRF 2008 (978 1 84101 545 3)

Day One: Blast off!

Turning

In our story today, Peter turned to Jesus and became one of his closest friends. Help the *Starship Discovery* turn on to the right path and find its way through space!

Give Peter and his friends a splash of colour!

Day One: Blast off!

Turning

Complete today's memory verse—and then see if you can memorize it!

Choose _ _ _ _ _ _ _ _ t_ _ _ _ _ _ _ _ _ _ you

_ _ _ _ _ s_ _ _ _ _ ; as for _ _ _ , I _ _ _ _ _ serve

_ _ _ _ L_ _ _ .

(Based on Joshua 24:15)

Think of a time when you had to make a choice. Did you make a good choice or a bad choice? How could your choice have been different? What difference would it have made?

Write your answer, or draw a picture, in the space below.

Day Two: Beam me up!

Trusting

In our story today, Peter trusted Jesus when he was asked to do something that he could never have managed to do on his own. How many things can you find in the picture that we usually trust? Find one thing in the picture that we can't trust.

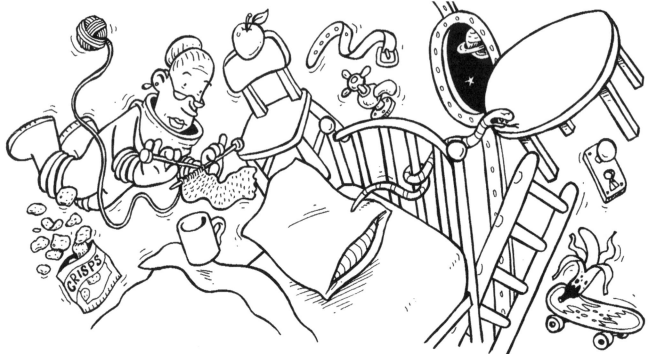

Colour in today's memory verse.

Trust in the Lord with all your heart

Proverbs 3:5

Day Two: Beam me up!

Trusting

You'll find the story of Peter walking on the water in Matthew 14:22–33. Read the story and then find all the words from the story in the wordsearch.

Jesus
disciples
boat
evening
ghost
waves
Peter
wind
walked
sink
save
hand
doubt
worshipped

T	A	O	B	T	R	D	E	K	L	A	W
B	E	S	T	W	J	I	V	N	T	U	E
U	L	O	I	R	E	D	A	W	I	T	D
O	H	N	A	L	S	L	S	Y	O	E	U
D	D	R	H	E	U	A	R	T	P	A	N
D	N	L	D	I	S	C	I	P	L	E	S
E	A	A	N	N	O	T	I	O	N	V	Y
O	H	U	R	G	O	H	W	N	U	E	N
D	E	R	H	S	S	T	A	S	I	N	K
N	D	O	I	R	N	G	P	R	O	I	U
E	S	R	O	B	S	C	W	H	A	N	P
T	T	W	E	R	T	U	A	R	E	G	E
W	E	T	V	E	R	S	V	E	F	T	V
R	F	S	E	M	E	R	E	T	E	P	M
S	O	R	O	R	Y	V	S	E	R	S	E

Try to imagine what it would be like to be Peter.

How do you think you would feel?_____
_____

Would you trust Jesus as much as Peter did? _____

Who do you trust most? _____

Who do you think trusts you most?_____

What does it mean to trust in God?_____
_____

Reproduced with permission from *The Starship Discovery Holiday Club!* published by BRF 2008 (978 1 84101 545 3)

Day Three: Black hole!

Tripping

Draw a picture of the *Starship Discovery* being sucked towards a black hole.

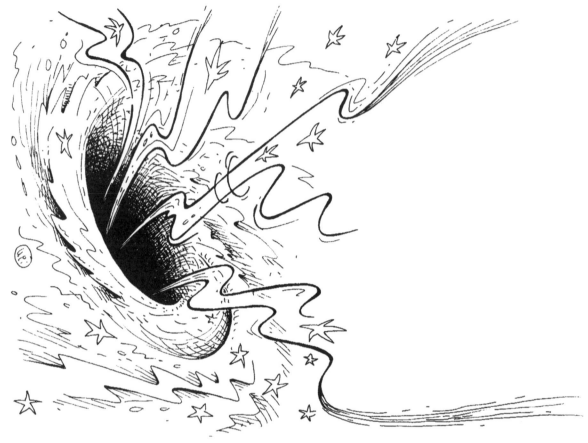

When we are frightened, we can talk to God. Write your prayer here and then, if you want to, share it with someone you trust.

Day Three: Black hole!

Tripping

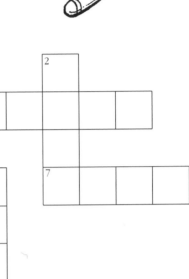

In our story today, Jesus is arrested and condemned to death.
Complete the crossword by using the clues below.

Across

3. Peter said he didn't know him.
5. Jesus died on this.
7. The sign above Jesus' head read _____ of the Jews.
8. What do we call talking to God?
9. This word means to disown or refuse to acknowledge.

Down

1. Jesus did this for us.
2. Crowing bird.
4. Someone who recognized Peter.
6. Peter said _____ times that he didn't know Jesus.
9. When Jesus died, the sky turned _____ .

Rearrange the words to find today's memory verse.

into came the save Christ to sinners world Jesus. (1 Timothy 1:15)

_____

Reproduced with permission from *The Starship Discovery Holiday Club!* published by BRF 2008 (978 1 84101 545 3)

Day Four: Breakthrough!

Transforming

At the space station, you need to visit all the fuel ports once only. Can you find the way?

Put your name where the thumb is, then say this memory verse using your hand.

God will never leave

Day Four: Breakthrough!

Transforming

Draw Peter and the other disciples before the Holy Spirit came.
Then draw a picture of them after the Holy Spirit had come.

Before	**After**

Transform this picture by colouring in all the shapes containing the letter 'o' to find out who God sent to be with us.

Day Five: Battle stations!

Training

In our story today, Peter was released from prison by an angel. Colour in the picture of Peter in prison. Can you see the angel?

Unscramble the letters in bold to find today's memory verse.

We often **ruffes**, but we are never **druches**. Even when we don't **wonk** what to do, we never **vegi** up. In times of **loubert**, God is with us, and when we are **codnekk** down, we get up **ingaa**.

2 Corinthians 4:8–9

We often _____, but we are never _____.

Even when we don't _____ what to do, we never

_____ up. In times of _____, God is with us,

and when we are _____ down, we get up _____.

2 Corinthians 4:8–9

give
again
trouble
crushed
knocked
know
suffer

Day Five: Battle stations!

Training

Spot ten differences between the two pictures.

Fill in the words on the grid.

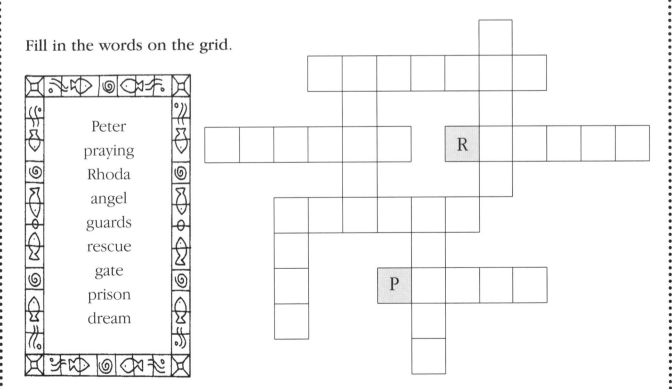

Peter
praying
Rhoda
angel
guards
rescue
gate
prison
dream

Appendix One

Material for a special service or evening event

The following pages contain extra ingredients for a special holiday club Sunday service or evening event. Don't forget to include some of the songs and Bible memory verses that the children have learnt, but please remember to add all the songs used during the holiday club on to your Christian Copyright Licence (CCL) list.

Starship Discovery space parade

Invite the children to bring along the crafts that they have made, such as their backpack oxygen bottles, kaleidoscopes, memory verse rockets, breakthrough spinners, salt dough stars and *Starship Discovery* memory rockets. (See pages 33–35 for details.) Announce that there will be a special parade when they will wear and carry the crafts they have made during the week. Do announce this several times during the week so that the children remember: a parade without models just doesn't work.

Have some suitable background music and an announcer with a microphone. Work out a catwalk for the children to parade around. You may choose to split the children into groups to make it easier to walk around. Use the following script.

Announcer: Welcome to our Starship Discovery parade!

The first group of children enter and parade around like models.

Announcer: As you can see, our space cadets are modelling very stylish backpack oxygen bottles. These are an essential item for anyone wanting to explore outer space. They are not needed on earth, of course, as—just like God—life-giving air is all around us. Let's give our space cadets a round of applause.

The first group of children exits and the next group enters.

Announcer: Next let me draw your attention to the dashing kaleidoscopes our space cadets are carrying. They know how important it is to focus on Jesus. Well done, guys!

Let's give our gallant space cadets a round of applause and welcome the next group.

The second group of children exits and the next group enters.

Announcer: Here comes our next group of space cadets, holding the very hip and trendy salt dough stars. Space cadets know that God made the stars and planets and that they themselves are God's special stars. Let's give them a round of applause.

The third group of children exits and the next group enters.

Announcer: Our next group of space cadets are demonstrating the very stylish breakthrough spinners. Our cadets have been learning that Jesus promises to be with us always—just as he was always with Peter and the rest of his disciples. Let's see those spinners spin, guys and girls! *(The children demonstrate their breakthrough spinners.)* Now give our space cadets a round of applause.

The fourth group of children exits and the next group enters.

Announcer: And finally, here comes our last group of space cadets, carrying their *Starship Discovery* memory rockets. Space cadets have been finding out that life is a journey of discovery and that the Bible— the word of God—is the best guide ever.

All the children come back to parade their crafts.

Announcer: Let's give all our space cadets a big round of applause and pray for them as they continue in their quest to live their lives in the way that God wants them to.

> **Cast**
>
> Narrator (reporter), Grandma Watt, Wendy, Rick, Mummy Watt, Herbert Tarragon
>
> **Props**
>
> A microphone (for the narrator), a walking stick (for Grandma Watt) and the Watt family theme tune (see page 14 for details).

Narr: *(Posing as a TV reporter, full of enthusiasm and energy)* There is great excitement here at the *Starship Discovery* landing pad. The crowds are going wild. I said, 'going wild' *(encouraging everyone to cheer)*. Reports are coming in to say that those intrepid explorers, the Watt family, have just landed after a successful mission into outer space.

Play the Watt Family theme tune.

Narr: Here they come now! *(Wendy walks in, arm in arm with Herbert Tarragon)* Wendy, can I have a quick word?

Wendy: A quick word—ha! They say I talk a lot, but I don't really talk a lot. I only talk if nobody else is talking, and then I may as well talk, because there's no point in everybody being quiet, is there?

Narr: *(Amazed)* Wow! Now I know why they made you the communications officer. So, Wendy, what actually happened?

Wendy: Well, we went into outer space, but we accidentally transported Mum to the alien Tarragon spaceship. We managed to contact the Tarragons, but they didn't want to give Mum back because their spaceship had never been so tidy.

Narr: *(Interrupts, looking at Herbert Tarragon)* So you managed to capture an alien? Get him!

Narrator chases Herbert Tarragon around in a figure of eight. Play chase music while this is going on. Enter Grandma. She trips up the reporter with her walking stick.

Grandma: Stop that! This is Herbert Tarragon—he's our new friend.

Narr: New friend?

Enter Rick.

Rick: Yeah! Space was radical! We saw lots of different planets and aliens. The computer guided us on an adventure of a lifetime.

Grandma: Yes, but it wasn't all good. We ended up in a black hole.

Narr: Gosh! What was that like?

Grandma: Black! *(Pause for response)* In fact, it was very black and very bleak. We thought we would be there for ever *(she looks down in the dumps)*, but then the Tarragons came alongside and helped us through this tough time *(she gives Herbert a beaming smile)*.

Narr: *(To Mummy Watt)* So, Mummy Watt! What have you discovered from your trip in space?

Mummy: Well, I've discovered that outer space is very big. In fact, it's bigger than big—it's huge. In fact, it's huger than huge—it just goes on and on. God did a great job when he made the universe. But it could do with a good tidy up.

Narr: *(To Herbert)* And what have you discovered about humans?

Herbert: *(Looking at Wendy)* Their bodies are very well put together.

Wendy: *(Looking shy)* Herbert, you don't say that sort of thing!

Herbert: Oh, sorry! Humans are very strange and eat shepherds in their pies. But, although they are very different from us Tarragons, they are very special too. It'll be great if we can learn to live in unity.

Narr: Yes, indeed! *(To Grandma)* Well, Grandma Watt, are the Watt family planning any more adventures?

Grandma: Life is just one big adventure.

Rick: Yeah, so much to learn, so much to discover.

Grandma: I'm sure there will be many more Watt family adventures to come.

Narr: (To audience) Well, we look forward to hearing all about them, don't we, folks? Thank you to my guests, the Watt family, and to everyone for tuning in. Tune in again soon! Goodbye for now.

Play the Watt Family theme tune as the cast all exit, dancing and singing as they go.

Family quiz

This can be a fun, interactive item for everyone to enjoy. In each category, the first question is for the children and the second question is for the adults.

Geography

1. Where would you find Blackpool Tower? (*Blackpool*)
2. Where would you find Leeds Castle? (*Near Maidstone in Kent*)

Maths

1. What's 1 + 2 + 3 + 4? (*10*)
2. What's 1 x 2 x 3 x 4? (*24*)

Spelling

1. Spell 'David'.
2. Spell 'Nebuchadnezzar'.

The Bible

1. How old was King Josiah on his eighth birthday? (*Eight*)
2. How long did Noah stay inside the big fish? (*It was Jonah who was swallowed by the fish*)

Bible story summary

```
Cast
Narrator and two others (A and B).
```

Narr: This week we've been on an adventure of discovery—with the *Starship Discovery*.

A: We've learnt about Peter's amazing adventure of discovery.

B: It all started when he met Jesus.

Narr: Jesus came walking along the shore of Lake Galilee and found Simon Peter and his friends looking after their nets. Simon Peter was a tough, rough fisherman… *(A mimes flexing muscles)* … who knew all there was to know about fishing *(B mimes casting nets and pulling them in)*. When Jesus chose Simon Peter to be his friend, Peter didn't hesitate—he turned around and followed Jesus. The adventure had begun.

A: *(Excitedly)* He saw Jesus feed over five thousand people with just five loaves and two small fish.

B: *(Even more excitedly)* Yeah, and he saw Jesus walking on water. When Jesus commanded Peter to do the same, he didn't hesitate—he jumped straight out of the boat and started walking on the water, too. Peter trusted Jesus.

Narr: Peter realized that Jesus was the Son of God.

A: *(Sadly)* But he let Jesus down and ran away.

B: *(Even more sadly)* He wept as his best friend was taken away to die on the cross.

Narr: *(Excitedly)* But then he jumped *(jumps)* for joy when he saw Jesus alive again. Jesus had conquered death. He truly is the King of kings and Lord of lords!

A: Peter saw Jesus raised up and was there when Jesus went back to heaven.

B: A little while later, Peter experienced the power of the Holy Spirit.

Narr: Peter became the leader of the early church. Now, two thousand years later, there are millions of churches and God's people are everywhere.

A: What a life!

B: What an adventure!

Narr: When Peter chose to follow Jesus, his life changed for ever and ever. And now Peter is in heaven…

A: … with his best friend…

B: … his Saviour and King.

Narr: We, too, can choose to turn around and follow Jesus—the King of kings—for ever and ever. We, too, can choose a life of discovery.

A and B: And, when we do, life will never be the same again!

Reproduced with permission from *The Starship Discovery Holiday Club!* published by BRF 2008 (978 1 84101 545 3)

Appendix Two

Starship Discovery badges

Use the templates below to make badges for the children. Photocopy on to thin card and attach a safety pin to the back with a strip of masking tape. The children can colour in their own badges and write their names in the space. Younger children might need team leaders to help them write their names.

Starship Discovery invitation cards

Photocopy the template below to make invitation cards for your *Starship Discovery!* holiday club. The children can colour them in and give them out to their friends and classmates.

Come along to the

Starship Discovery!

Holiday Club

You are warmly invited to our Starship Discovery! Holiday Club

At _____

On _____

From _____

Telephone to book your place!

. . . .

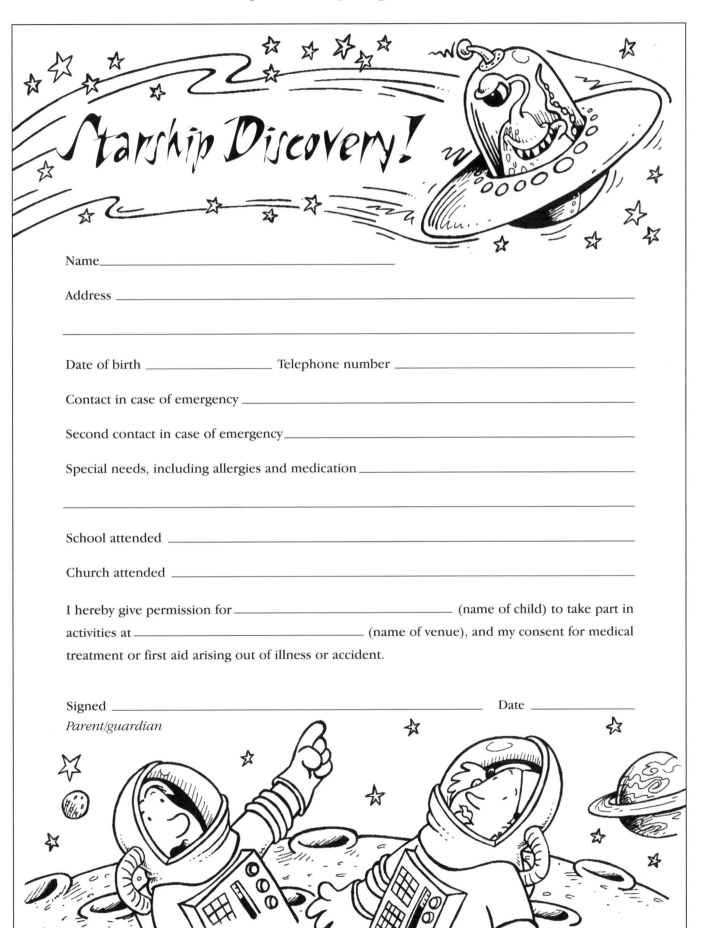

Name

Address

Date of birth _____ Telephone number _____

Contact in case of emergency _____

Second contact in case of emergency_____

Special needs, including allergies and medication _____

School attended _____

Church attended _____

I hereby give permission for _____ (name of child) to take part in

activities at _____ (name of venue), and my consent for medical

treatment or first aid arising out of illness or accident.

Signed _____ Date _____
Parent/guardian

Reproduced with permission from *The Starship Discovery Holiday Club!* published by BRF 2008 (978 1 84101 545 3)

Starship Discovery! presentation poster

Use this poster to invite parents, relatives and friends to a *Starship Discovery!* event
to find out what the children have been doing during their holiday club week.

Starship Discovery! memory verse templates

Photocopy the templates below and stick the verses on to the fins of your *memory verse rocket* (see page 34)

✂

Memory verse:
Choose yourself today whom you will serve;
as for me, I will serve the Lord.

✂

Memory verse:
I will always be with you;
I will never abandon you.

✂

Memory verse:
Trust in the Lord with all your heart and lean
not on your own understanding.

✂

Memory verse:
We often suffer, but we are never crushed.
Even when we don't know what to do,
we never give up. In times of trouble,
God is with us, and when we are knocked
down, we get up again.

✂

Memory verse:
Christ Jesus came into the world
to save sinners.

Appendix Three

Time fillers and extra games

Quick activities

Design a logo

You might like to think about designing a logo for your team, or an overall logo for your *Starship Discovery!* holiday club. Your ideas might include different stars and planets, features such as Saturn's rings or Jupiter's satellites, comet tails, shooting stars, double stars, polar lights, or the Milky Way. You should also include your team name.

Word busters

Give the children sheets of paper with a word written at the top. They have to see how many words they can make out of the key word, using the letters once only in each word, and not using plurals or proper nouns.

Suggested word list for younger children:
• Trusting
• Teleport
• Tarragon
• Computer
• Starship

Suggested word list for older children:
• Turn around
• Spaceship
• Transformation
• Breakthrough
• Battle stations

Suggested word for everyone:
• Starship Discovery

Quick games

Alien splat

Get the children to stand in a circle, with a leader in the middle. Explain that the leader is an alien from outer space, armed with a 'splat gun'. The splat gun is the index finger of his or her right (or left) hand.

The leader turns on the spot and points the splat gun at random at one of the children, exclaiming 'Splat!' as he or she does so. The child sits down as fast as possible. The two children on either side of the child who has sat down then fire their splat guns (index fingers) at each other. The child to shout 'Splat!' first remains in the game, while the child who was slower is out of the game and sits down on the spot. Meanwhile, the child who was originally targeted by the leader stands up and remains in the game.

The leader then turns on the spot in the centre of the circle, ready to 'splat' another child. The game continues with children sitting down when they are 'out'. As more children become 'out' and are sitting down, the remaining children have to keep alert to work out who is on either side when a child targeted by the leader drops to the ground. This becomes less and less easy, because the children on either side of the targeted child will not be immediately next to them.

The last two children left in the game have a 'splatters at dawn' shootout in which they stand back to back in the centre of the circle and, on command from the leader, walk slowly away from each other. On the command 'Splat!' they then have to turn and 'splat' each other. The child to turn and shout 'Splat!' first wins the game and gets a point for their team.

Shooting stars

This is similar to the classic game 'Yes and no'. Ask for a volunteer and interview them. All they are allowed to say in reply is 'Shooting stars'.

The interview could go something like this: 'What's your name? What did you have for breakfast? Dinner? Tea? What shampoo do you use? What football team do you support? What do I look like?' To all of these questions, the volunteer has to reply 'Shooting stars' without smiling or laughing. Set a time limit to the game and award the volunteer a point for their team if they manage to keep going without a mistake (or smiling or laughing) to the end of the time limit.

Herbert says

Play the classic game 'Simon Says', but use the name 'Herbert' instead, or invite a child to be 'Herbert'.

Grandma Watt went shopping

Sit the children in a circle. The leader says, 'Grandma Watt went shopping and she bought…' (an item beginning with the letter 'A'). The child next to the leader then says, 'Grandma Watt went shopping and she bought…' He or she repeats the item the leader has chosen and adds another item, beginning with the letter 'B'. The game continues around the circle, each child repeating the previous items and adding an item of their own beginning with the next letter of the alphabet. If a child is unable to remember Grandma Watt's shopping list, they are out of the game. The game continues until there is only one child left. Award the winner a point for their team.

Alien skittles

Put the children into their teams, making sure that the teams are of equal size. Give each team six plastic cups. Stack the cups for each team at the opposite end of the playing area, with three on the bottom row, two on the middle row and one on the top. Have a leader stationed at each stack.

You will need a nylon stocking and a small soft ball for each team. Drop the ball into the toe of the stocking. The children take it in turns to put the stocking on their head and run down the course. They then have to knock down the stack of cups by swinging the ball in the stocking. They are not allowed to touch the stocking with their hands.

When each child has knocked down the stack, they run back up the playing area and give the stocking to the next person in their team. Meanwhile, the leader stationed by the cups restacks them in readiness for the next player. When all the children in the team have had a turn, the team sits down. The first team to sit down wins the game and is awarded a team point.

Clusters

Put the children into their teams (clusters). Place each team in a different part of the playing area, the same distance away from the leader, who sits on a chair in the centre. The leader calls out an item that the children are likely to have somewhere within their team, such as a blue sock, a pink hairband or a belt. The child in each team who possesses that item runs and gives it to the leader. The first child to do so wins a team point.

The game continues until the leader has called ten or twelve items. Have a second leader to keep a tally of the points scored by each team. The winning team is the one with the most points at the end of the game. Suggested items are a left shoe, a right shoe, a comb, a coin, a watch, a clean tissue, a ring, a red T-shirt and so on.

Appendix Four

Further resources and training events

Music

The Junior Heroes! DVD

Action Packed Praise 2
Produced by John Hardwick and ACM Studios, see the songs in action and sing along too. The DVD includes:

* *Junior Heroes!* theme song
* Bible memory verse songs
* Bible narrations performed by John Hardwick
* A selection of further popular songs by John Hardwick

Available from: www.johnhardwick.org.uk

High-energy Holiday Club Songs

Easy-to-sing action songs for Bible-based kids

Specially written and composed to support the material in John's two holiday club resource books *We're going on a Jungle Jamboree* and *Champions!* (both published by Barnabas). Includes all the songs and backing tracks from both holiday club programmes.
High-energy Holiday Club Songs CD is published by Barnabas, price £8.99. Available from:

BRF
15 The Chambers
Vineyard
Abingdon OX14 3FE
Telephone: 01865 319700
Fax: 01865 319701
E-mail: enquiries@brf.org.uk
Website: www.brf.org.uk

Stay legal
Please remember to tick any songs used during your holiday club or in your weekly church services on your Christian Copyright Licence (CCL) list.

Training events

John Hardwick also offers a range of training events, including:

* **Training sessions**: A host of ideas with a particular focus on storytelling and music for anyone involved in leading services and events where children are present.
* **Praise parties**: High-energy, fast-moving sessions for primary-aged kids.
* **New songs sessions**: A chance to see John's infectious songs in action.
* **All-age services**: Plenty of variety with a message for everyone.
* **Holiday clubs**: John offers a fun-packed holiday club package including stage-based presentations, songs, Bible narrations and puppetry.

For further information about any of the above products or events, please contact:

John Hardwick
2 Lucketts Close
Histon
Cambridge
CB24 9HG

Telephone: 01223 235106
E-mail: johnhardwick36@hotmail.com
Website: www.johnhardwick.org.uk

Schools work

John is a member of BRF's *Barnabas* team and offers full-day RE presentations, bringing the Bible to life through the creative arts, including music, creative storytelling, puppetry and circus skills. A typical day with John might include:

* A 20-minute assembly with the theme 'Working together and valuing one another'. The assembly includes a juggling talk, song and Bible story told in a dramatic way and is suitable for collective worship across Key Stages 1 and 2.
* A 40- to 50-minute assembly with the theme 'Creation

appreciation', leading into an exploration of our uniqueness and how we need to show respect and compassion for others. This is John's most popular theme and could be shortened for younger years. The presentation includes Bible stories told in a dramatic way, a creative poem, a puppet sketch, music and songs, a juggling story with a diabolo, questions and plenty of participation. Ideally, the presentation needs to take place in the school hall or similar space. The material is designed to meet the needs of different year groups across Key Stages 1 and 2 and could be repeated with each year group as required.

- A 30-minute class or year group presentation exploring the value of books and the Bible. This includes a Bible story told in a dramatic way, a puppet sketch, song, juggling, unicycling and other circus skills. Ideally, the presentation needs to take place in the school hall or similar space. The material is designed to meet the needs of different year groups across Key Stages 1 and 2 and will be repeated with each year group as required.

- A 'circus skills' workshop suitable for Years 5 and 6. The workshop offers the opportunity for pupils to try their hand at skills such as juggling, plate-spinning, stunt sticks and diabolos. Maximum number per group: 30 children.

To book John for a *Barnabas* RE day, or for further details, contact:

BRF
15 The Chambers
Vineyard
Abingdon
OX14 3FE

Telephone: 01865 319700
Fax: 01865 319701
E-mail: enquiries@brf.org.uk
Website: www.barnabasinchurches.org.uk

Puppet suppliers

Children Worldwide

Full range of puppets and other children's resources.

Children Worldwide
Dalesdown
Honeybridge Lane
Dial Post
Horsham
RH13 8NX
Telephone: 01403 711032
Website: www.childrenworldwide.co.uk

Hands up for God

People, animal and biblical character puppets plus other related resources and ministry events.

Hands up for God Ministries
34 Holbourne Close
Barrow-upon-Soar
LE12 8NE
Telephone: 01509 415129
E-mail: dennis@handsupforgod.com
Website: www.handsupforgod.com

One Way UK

A full range of puppets.

One Way UK
Unit 6, Britten Road
Robert Court Industrial Estate
Elgar Road South
Reading
RG2 0AU
Telephone: 0845 490 1929
Email: info@onewayuk.com
Website: www.onewayuk.com

★ ★ ★ ★ ★ ★ ★

Holiday club resources

By John Hardwick

978 1 84101 253 7, £7.99

We're going on a Jungle Jamboree! introduces five key parables from Luke's Gospel, exploring the message behind the story in a contemporary, relevant and fun way. The stories are placed into a jungle setting, taking the child on a journey of adventure on the different routes through life. Each day comprises Bible story narration, serial drama/adventure story, puppet sketches, quick quizzes, jungle games and crafts, action songs with music notation, and differentiated fun sheets. Photocopy permission is included. All the songs are included on the *High-Energy Holiday Club Songs* CD (see page 71 for details).

★ ★ ★ ★ ★ ★ ★

Holiday club resources

By John Hardwick

978 1 84101 185 1, £8.99

Champions! uses the analogy of the Olympic Games to explore how Jesus 'ran the race' for God. It is designed to encourage children also to run that race, running straight towards the goal and finishing the race in order to win the ultimate prize of eternal life. This is the prize that God offers to each one of us through the work of his Son, Christ Jesus.

This book includes songs, theme illustrations, daily dramas, puppet sketches, Bible stories, quizzes, crafts, games and fun sheets for younger and older children. Photocopy permission is included. All the songs are included on the *High-Energy Holiday Club Songs* CD (see page 71 for details).

★ ★ ★ ★ ★ ★ ★

Holiday club resources

By John Hardwick

978 1 84101 460 9, £8.99

The world of entertainment has always featured superheroes to inspire and enthral children. The Bible, too, has its heroes, many of whom are children and young people who trusted God and made a real difference in the face of adversity. As a holiday club, junior church programme, midweek club or as part of all-age worship, junior heroes of today can explore the heroic exploits of courageous junior heroes in the Bible.

★ ★ ★ ★ ★ ★ ★

Other resources

from Barnabas

Footsteps
to the Feast

12 two-hour children's programmes
for Christian festivals and special times
of the year

Ideal for
6–10s

Martyn Payne

Foreword by Mary Hawes,
National Children's Officer for the Church of England

978 1 84101 464 7, £8.99

These two-hour programmes are ideal for special events or after-school clubs, picking up on Christian festivals and special days of the year. Experienced children's worker Martyn Payne provides background information for each festival, with warm-up activities, Bible basis, ideas for storytelling, drama, music crafts and prayers. While all the component parts of the programme are important, the primary aim is to share God's word with children and provide an opportunity to come close to God in worship.

★ ★ ★ ★ ★ ★ ★

Other resources

from Barnabas

978 1 84101 503 3, £8.99

Bursting with ideas to draw people of all ages together and help them experience Christian community outside of Sunday worship. The resource book contains 15 themed programme outlines, with ideas for creative art and craft activities, recipes and family-friendly worship. *Messy Church* creates the opportunity for parents, carers and children to express their creativity, sit down together for a meal, experience worship and have fun in a church context.

★ ★ ★ ★ ★ ★ ★

Other resources

from Barnabas

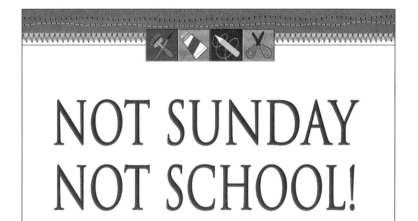

978 1 84101 490 6, £9.99

This book sets out to show that, with a bit of lateral and creative thinking, even the smallest church can run vibrant and successful children's groups. Packed with ideas and activities for an alternative model to the traditional Sunday school, the book provides ten 2-hour workshop programmes, an alternative programme for Hallowe'en and a series of 5-day holiday club programmes or stand-alone workshops for the summer months. Material includes arts and crafts, drama, cookery, Bible teaching and worship, all of which have been thoroughly field-tested in the author's own benefice in Buckinghamshire. Ideal for small churches.

Resourcing people to work with 3–11s

in churches and schools

- Articles, features, ideas
- Training and events
- Books and resources
- www.barnabasinchurches.org.uk

Barnabas is an imprint of brf

BRF is a Registered Charity

 Have you signed up to receive the Barnabas monthly email?
To receive mailings about *Barnabas* resources and services, sign up at:

www.barnabasinchurches.org.uk